Welcome to
Windows® 7

GREG P. MARSHALL II
Whatcom Community College

DAN MARSHALL-CAMPBELL
Whatcom Community College

LABYRINTH
LEARNING

El Sobrante, CA

President:
Brian Favro

Acquisitions Editor:
Jason Favro

Managing Editor:
Laura A. Lionello

Production Manager:
Rad Proctor

eLearning Production Manager:
Arl S. Nadel

Editorial Team:
Donna Bacidore, Eddie T. Bryant, and
Sandy Jones

Indexing:
Afterwords Editorial Services

Cover Design:
Huckdesign

LABYRINTH
LEARNING™

Welcome to Windows 7
by Greg P. Marshall II and Dan Marshall-Campbell

Copyright © 2010 by Labyrinth Learning

Labyrinth Learning
P.O. Box 20820
El Sobrante, California 94803
800.522.9746
On the web at lablearning.com

ITEM: 1-59136-292-X
ISBN-13: 978-1-59136-292-0

Manufactured in the United States of America.

Globus 0 9 8 7 6 5 4 3 2

Welcome to
Windows 7

Table of Contents

UNIT 1

Windows 7 Basics

LESSON 1

Getting Your First Look. 3

LESSON 2

Starting Programs 31

LESSON 3

Working with a Program . . 65

UNIT 2
File Management

LESSON 4
Finding Files 107

LESSON 5
Storing Files 135

Preface

What Is Covered: *Welcome to Windows® 7* is a complete introduction to Microsoft's new operating system. In Unit 1, students begin their exploration of Windows 7 and general computer concepts. They start programs, learn multitasking techniques, and create and save files in Paint and WordPad. In Unit 2, students deal with file management. They learn how files, folders, and drives are organized on the computer, as well as how to create, organize, and manage their own folders. Students even learn how to copy files to CDs, DVDs, and USB flash drives. In Unit 3, students connect to the Internet and learn how to customize Windows 7's look to suit their needs and preferences. Throughout this book we have also included Behind the Screen sections, which are brief discussions on topics such as computer components, file storage, and social media sites.

What Is Different: For more than a decade, Labyrinth has been working to perfect our *unique instructional design*. The benefit of our approach is that learning is faster and easier for students. Instructors have found that our approach works well in self-paced, instructor-led, and "blended" learning environments. The Labyrinth approach has many key features, including the following:

- *Concise concept discussions* followed by Hands-On exercises that give students experience with those concepts right away.

- *Figures* are always in close context with the text so no figure numbers are necessary.

- *Quick Reference* sections summarize key tasks with generic steps that will work without repeating an exercise. These can be particularly useful during open-book tests.

- *Hands-On exercises* are carefully written and repeatedly tested to be absolutely reliable. Many exercise steps are illustrated with figures to make them easier to follow.

- *Skill Builder exercises* provide additional practice on key skills using less detailed exercise steps as the student progresses through the lesson.

We are now expanding our book list by adapting this approach to teaching other application programs, including Intuit® QuickBooks®, Adobe Photoshop Elements®, Macromedia® Dreamweaver®, digital photography, and more.

Comprehensive Support: This course is also supported on the Labyrinth website with a comprehensive instructor support package that includes detailed lesson plans, PowerPoint presentations, a course syllabus, extensive test banks, and more. Our unique WebSims allow students to perform realistic exercises with the web, email, and application program tasks that would be difficult to set up in a computer lab.

We are grateful to the many instructors who have used Labyrinth titles and suggested improvements to us over the years we have been writing and publishing books. *Welcome to Windows 7* has benefited greatly from the reviewing and suggestions of John Bullock, Kirkwood Community College (Marion, IA); Vicky Kelder, Westchester Community College (Congers, NY); Nikkea Masters, Placer School for Adults (Auburn, CA); Chesty Peterson, Downey Adult School (Downey, CA); Joseph Roy, Madison Area Technical College (Madison, WI); and Judy Spencer, Central Oklahoma Juvenile Center (Tecumseh, OK).

How This Book Is Organized

The information in this book is presented so that you master the fundamental skills first, and then build on those skills as you work with the more comprehensive topics.

Visual Conventions

This book uses many visual and typographical cues to guide you through the lessons. This page provides examples and described the functions of each cue.

Type this text	Anything you should type at the keyboard is printed in this typeface.
TIP!	Tips, Notes, and Warnings are used throughout the text to draw attention to certain topics.
Command→ Command	This convention indicates multiple selections to be made from a menu bar. For example, File→Save means to select File, and then to select Save.
Command→ Command→ Command, etc.	This convention indicates how to give a command from the Ribbon. The commands are written: Ribbon Tab→Command Group→ Command→Subcommand.
From the Keyboard	Quick Reference tables provide generic instructions for key tasks. Only perform these tasks if you are instructed to in an exercise.
QUICK REFERENCE	Quick Reference tables provide generic instructions for key tasks. Only perform these tasks if you are instructed to in an exercise.
On the **Web**	Supplementary information available on the web page for this book is highlighted with this icon. Visit the web page periodically for helpful tips and content.
	Hands-On exercises are introduced immediately after concept discussions. They provide detailed, step-by-step tutorials so you can master the skills presented.

The Concepts Review section includes both true/false and multiple choice questions designed to gauge your understanding of concepts.

 Skill Builder exercises provide additional hands-on practice with moderate assistance.

 Try This at Home exercises test your skills by describing the correct results without providing specific instructions on how to achieve them.

Windows 7 Basics

In this unit, you will begin your exploration of Microsoft's newest operating system, Windows 7. You will begin by starting the computer, navigating the Desktop, practicing your mouse skills, and shutting down the computer. You will also launch programs from the Start menu and work with multitasking skills. Finally, in this unit you will create, edit, and save documents in Paint and WordPad.

Getting Your First Look

Windows 7 is the newest version of Microsoft's Windows operating system. With this release, Microsoft continues with its goal of making access to the functionality of the computer easier and less frustrating for the new computer user. As you work through this lesson, you will have the opportunity to learn and practice starting a computer using Windows 7, navigating basic features of the opening screen known as the Desktop, using mouse skills necessary to navigate in Windows 7, and properly shutting down the computer.

LESSON OBJECTIVES

After studying this lesson, you will be able to:

- Log on to the computer using a user-name and a password
- Describe the basic layout of the Windows 7 Desktop screen
- Use the right-click and dragging mouse motions
- Shut down the computer correctly
- Add, move, and remove Gadgets

*Additional learning resources are available at **labpub.com/learn/silver/wtw7***

Case Study: Starting Something New

Alberta moved into her son's home. Her son, Ted, wanted Alberta to have access to the family computer. He thought she could play games such as Solitaire, learn to use email, and search the Internet. To give Alberta privacy, her son set up a separate username and password.

Alberta was scared the first time she sat down at the computer, but Ted said, "Push the power button and start using it. And don't worry; you won't break anything." Her son explained the logon screen and showed her how to enter her password.

When another colorful screen appeared, Ted said, "That's the Desktop. Here is an icon for Solitaire. It's like a light switch to start the game. Put your mouse pointer over the top of the icon and double-click; just click the left mouse button twice; click, click." Alberta double-clicked, and the game started. It looked just like the real game.

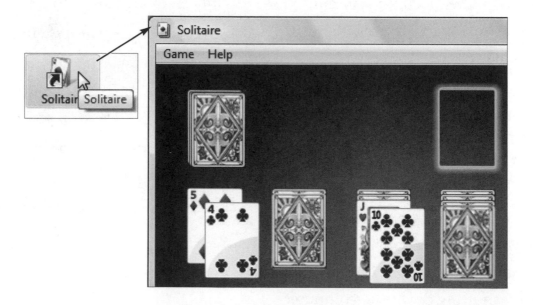

"Practice using your mouse by holding down the left button on a card, dragging it to the right place, and then releasing the button to drop it. And remember, don't worry about breaking anything!"

At first it was difficult, but after awhile, Alberta became more comfortable with the mouse and rarely had to look at it before she clicked. She began to think, "This computer is going to be fun."

Logging On to Windows

Most computer systems used in schools and businesses are networked together. An important part of network security is making sure everyone using computers on the network is authorized to do so. Logging on to the computer is the process of entering your username and password into the computer so that access can be granted.

Passwords

A critical piece of the login process is the password. Your password allows you into the computer. Passwords can contain upper- and lowercase letters as well as numbers and symbols. You must enter the password exactly as it was given to you.

 **WARNING!** None of your passwords should ever be shared. Sharing passwords is one of the top reasons people have computer and financial information stolen.

Creating Your Own Passwords

When you create your own passwords on a home or office computer, make sure they cannot be easily guessed. Don't use familiar names, birthdays, or common words. Following are some examples of good and poor passwords.

Good Passwords	Poor Passwords
!GreeN2	Fido
8ate8	Johndoe
Fun2Dr1v	12345678
AcEsn8s	Password

What Happens During the Startup Process?

From the moment you turn on the computer and throughout the login process, the computer and Windows 7 are working together to get ready for you. Windows 7 is not one giant program but a collection of hundreds of little programs. As the computer starts, various parts and pieces of Windows 7 are starting as well. Together they form the *operating system* that we see and work with on the screen.

 NOTE! Throughout the rest of this book, Windows 7 will be referred to as simply Win 7.

 HANDS-ON 1.1 **Log on to Win 7**

In this exercise, you will log on to your computer using the login name and password provided by the instructor.

1. If necessary, turn on the computer and monitor. (The computer may already be switched on in a computer lab.) Ask the instructor for help if you cannot locate the power buttons.

   After a pause, the computer begins starting up. This will usually take about a minute. When the startup process is complete, a login screen appears. If you are performing this exercise at home, a different screen will appear.

2. Follow the steps for your location to log on:

Computer Lab

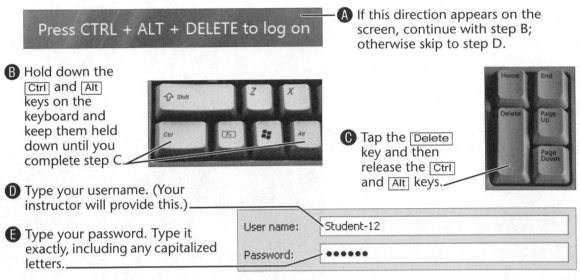

A If this direction appears on the screen, continue with step B; otherwise skip to step D.

Press CTRL + ALT + DELETE to log on

B Hold down the Ctrl and Alt keys on the keyboard and keep them held down until you complete step C.

C Tap the Delete key and then release the Ctrl and Alt keys.

D Type your username. (Your instructor will provide this.)

E Type your password. Type it exactly, including any capitalized letters.

User name: Student-12

Password: ●●●●●●

F Tap the Enter key or click the Enter button with your mouse.

The Win 7 Desktop appears. If your login name or password was not correct, you will be asked to reenter both again. Simply do so, paying close attention to typing the username and password correctly.

Home Computer

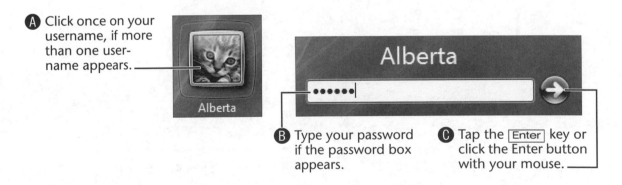

A Click once on your username, if more than one user-name appears.

Alberta

●●●●●●

B Type your password if the password box appears.

C Tap the Enter key or click the Enter button with your mouse.

The Win 7 Desktop appears. If your login password was not correct, you will be asked to reenter it again. Simply do so, paying close attention to typing the username and password correctly.

The Win 7 Desktop

Once you have logged on to the computer, you will be looking at the Win 7 Desktop. The Desktop is the primary work area in Win 7, and like your desk at school, everything you work on is placed in this area.

The Desktop has many unique features that help you be more efficient in using the computer.

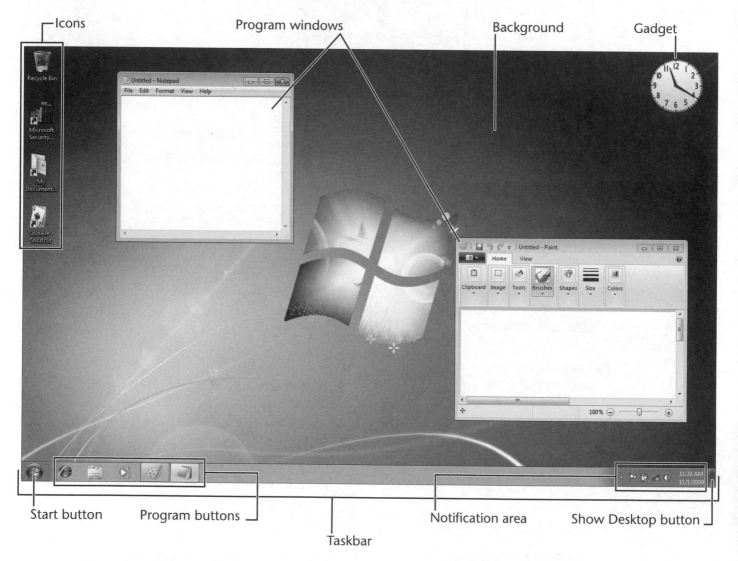

This is what the Win 7 Desktop looks like with some common features displayed.

Start Button The round button in the bottom-left corner of the screen displaying the Windows logo is called the Start button. Access to most of Win 7's features, your software, and your documents starts from this button. Microsoft wants you to remember that everything "starts" with this little round button.

Icons   Icons are small pictures on the screen that represent programs or other features. You can launch these programs and features by double-clicking on their icons. In the previous illustration, you will notice an icon in the upper-left corner labeled Recycle Bin. This represents the Recycle Bin folder, where files are moved when deleted (as discussed later in this book).

Typical Win 7 icons

Notification Area   The Notification Area is located on the taskbar in the bottom-right corner of the computer screen (see the previous illustration). The Notification Area contains icons for programs that are currently running but don't necessarily need a lot of user interaction. Programs listed here can include antivirus programs, Internet connection software, Microsoft Outlook email, and possibly the software that runs your printer.

 TIP!   If you point your mouse pointer over an icon in the Notification Area, a small dialog box called a ScreenTip will appear, telling you what that program does or is doing. ScreenTips are helpful if you're curious about what's going on in your computer.

Basic Computer Components

Your computer is a collection of hardware parts working together with Win 7 and other software applications. Knowing the name and function of various components can give you a better understanding of the computing process.

Processor   The *processor* is often referred to as the "brain" of the computer. The central processing unit (CPU) does all the processing that keeps programs running, moves the cards when you play Solitaire, and does the math in your spreadsheet programs. How quickly these processes are carried out is largely determined by the gigahertz (GHz) rating of the CPU. A larger GHz rating means the processor is capable of more billions of processing cycles per second.

Intel's Core 2 Duo is a popular processor for computers running Win 7.

Hard Drive   The hard drive is the permanent storage in the computer. Your files and the programs that run on the computer are stored on the hard drive. You can think of the hard drive as a large filing cabinet where all the files used on the computer are stored.

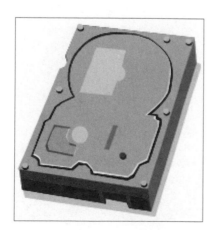

Random Access Memory Hard drives operate at a relatively slow speed, so your computer does not run programs directly from the hard drive. All of the programs run on the computer are first loaded into Random Access Memory (RAM) to take advantage of the very high speed at which data can be accessed by the CPU. As you edit a letter or make a drawing, the information is being stored in RAM. RAM is considered temporary memory because, unlike the hard drive, when the computer is turned off, all of the data in RAM is lost. A letter or drawing being stored in RAM will, at some point, need to be saved to permanent storage, or it will be lost when the computer is shut down.

Network Port The network port allows the computer to connect to a wired network of other computers and to shared resources such as printers, files, and the Internet.

At home, you may use the network port to connect your computer to *broadband* (high-speed) Internet services such as cable or Digital Subscriber Line (DSL).

Universal Serial Bus (USB) A USB port is the small rectangular port or connector now common on all computers. These USB ports allow you to connect various pieces of equipment to your computer using a single standardized cord and plug. Once a device is connected via the USB port, Win 7 will recognize the equipment and help with its configuration. Before USB, different equipment had special connectors and cables, and it was much more difficult for new users to set up their computers.

A typical USB port on the front of a computer

A cable on which you can plug in a USB device

Here's an example of a USB plug and port. Notice the universal symbol for USB on each.

Using a Mouse

The mouse is your main tool for controlling programs on the Win 7 Desktop. Moving the mouse controls the movements of a mouse pointer on the screen. The mouse should be held in your hand with your index finger resting lightly on or above the left mouse button. You may find that dragging your thumb on the mouse pad or your desktop as you move and click can help control the movement of the mouse.

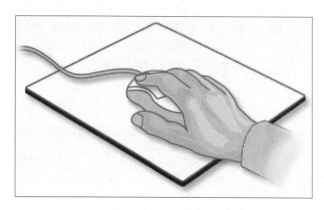

Make sure you are holding the mouse with your hand. Your index finger should be resting lightly on the left mouse button.

 NOTE! Make sure you keep your wrist straight when using the mouse. The top of the mouse should always point toward the top of the mouse pad. Don't steer the mouse like a car. Twisting or turning the mouse disorients the mouse pointer.

Mouse Motions

There are five basic actions that you can take with the mouse: point, click, drag, double-click, and right-click. With an understanding of these basic actions, you can control most features of Win 7 with the mouse.

Point   Pointing is holding the tip of the mouse pointer over an object on the screen. When pointing with the mouse, it is very important to keep your mouse steady so that your mouse pointer stays pointed on the correct screen item.

 TIP! Only the tip of the mouse cursor is active. The remainder of the mouse cursor is there to make the cursor easier to see.

Incorrect; tip
of pointer is
too low.

Incorrect; tip
of pointer is
too high.

Correct; tip of pointer
is over icon. Notice
how the icon is "lit up."

Click   A click or single-click is used when pushing on-screen buttons. This entails pushing the left mouse button one time. It is important when clicking that you hold the mouse still and click gently. If you wiggle the mouse while clicking, the computer may think you want to drag the object.

Drag   Dragging is used to move items around the screen. A drag works like a click except that you do not let go of the mouse button. Once you position your mouse pointer over the item you want to move, click and hold down the left mouse button until the Desktop item is in the new location, and then you can lift your finger off the button. This action is often referred to as *drag and drop*.

Double-Click   Double-clicking involves positioning the mouse over a Desktop item and clicking twice with the left mouse button. Double-clicking usually is used to start a program or to open a file or folder. As with clicking, it is important to hold the mouse still. If you wiggle the mouse when double-clicking, the computer might not open the item you clicked but instead might interpret the mouse movement as an attempt to drag the item.

NOTE!   Be patient if you are having trouble double-clicking. A double click does not have to be lightning fast. You have about a second to complete the two clicks. Slowing down your clicking speed will help keep you from wiggling the mouse.

Right-Click   Right-clicking is done with the right mouse button. Clicking with this button displays a pop-up menu. The choices on the menu will change depending on which Desktop object you have clicked. You will learn more about right-clicking later in this lesson.

TIP!   If you accidentally click on the right mouse button, a pop-up menu may appear on the screen. You can make the accidental menu disappear by clicking another place on the Desktop with the left mouse button or by tapping the ESC key in the upper-left corner of your keyboard.

HANDS-ON 1.2 **Practice Using the Mouse**

In this exercise, you will use the mouse to point, click, and drag the Recycle Bin on the Desktop.

1. Make sure the mouse is positioned on the desk so you can place your entire hand on the mouse as shown in the following illustration. Hold the mouse loosely so your hand is comfortable while you rest your fingers over the two mouse buttons.

2. Follow these steps to start using the mouse:

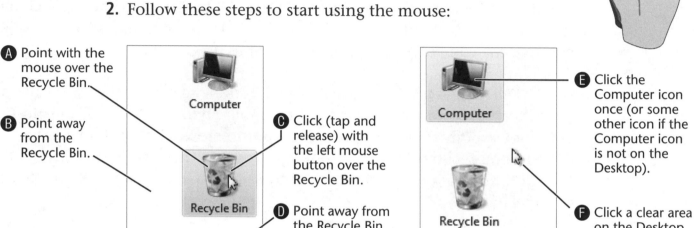

Ⓐ Point with the mouse over the Recycle Bin.

Ⓑ Point away from the Recycle Bin.

Computer

Recycle Bin

Ⓒ Click (tap and release) with the left mouse button over the Recycle Bin.

Ⓓ Point away from the Recycle Bin (don't click). Notice that it stays selected.

Computer

Recycle Bin

Ⓔ Click the Computer icon once (or some other icon if the Computer icon is not on the Desktop).

Ⓕ Click a clear area on the Desktop once to deselect the Computer (or other) icon.

3. Locate the Recycle Bin on your Desktop then hold your mouse pointer over the Recycle Bin and read the ScreenTip that appears.

4. Point at the Recycle Bin and single-click to select the icon. Notice the change in appearance when the icon is selected.

Practice Dragging

Dragging is a basic technique to move objects on the screen, select text, and perform many other tasks and commands.

5. Follow these steps to drag the Recycle Bin to a new location on the Desktop:

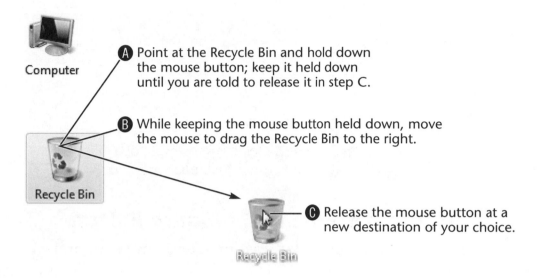

Computer

Ⓐ Point at the Recycle Bin and hold down the mouse button; keep it held down until you are told to release it in step C.

Ⓑ While keeping the mouse button held down, move the mouse to drag the Recycle Bin to the right.

Recycle Bin

Ⓒ Release the mouse button at a new destination of your choice.

Recycle Bin

6. Carefully drag the Recycle Bin back to its original location on the Desktop.

Using Gadgets

Gadgets are small productivity programs that can help put useful information at your fingertips. Gadgets can be a simple Desktop clock or more complicated programs that provide a picture slide show, the day's weather, or current news headlines.

The Clock is an example of a Gadget that comes installed with Win 7.

Clicking with the Right Mouse Button

The right mouse button is used frequently in Win 7 and within many programs to display helpful pop-up menus. These menus are context-sensitive. This means that the menu that appears will contain tasks related to the object on which you have clicked.

To display a pop-up menu, place the tip of the mouse pointer over an object (for example, a command in the Start menu) and click the right button on the mouse. When the pop-up menu appears, choose items from the menu with the left mouse button.

Right-clicking on the Desktop brings up a menu of commands related specifically to the Desktop. The Gadgets item on the menu will bring up a selection of Gadgets.

Standard Gadgets

- **Clock**—This Gadget is a standard clock used to tell time.

- **Slide Show (a picture viewer)**—This Gadget randomly scrolls through the sample pictures that are provided with Windows. It can be set to show your own pictures instead of samples.

- **Feed Headlines (an RSS reader)**—This Gadget is used by intermediate and advanced users to gather news stories from various sources on the Internet and compile them into one list for easy reading.

Adding, Removing, and Changing Gadgets

Gadgets are not permanently attached to the Desktop. They can be added or moved anywhere on the Desktop. If you no longer need a particular Gadget, it can be removed at any time.

Another Gadget feature is a small toolbar that appears when the mouse pointer hovers over a Gadget. It provides quick commands to close or change the Gadget's options and a handle to drag the Gadget.

 —The Close button lets you remove the Gadget.

The Options button lets you change the Gadget.

The Drag Gadget handle lets you move the Gadget.

A small toolbar with quick commands appears when you point at a Gadget.

QUICK REFERENCE: Using Gadgets

Task	Procedure
Add a new Gadget	• Right-click on the background of the Desktop and choose Gadgets from the pop-up menu. This will bring up the Gadget menu with a complete list of optional Gadgets.
Move a Gadget	• Position your mouse over the Gadget and then drop the Gadget anywhere on the Desktop.

Task	Procedure
Remove a Gadget	• Right-click on the Gadget and choose Close Gadget from the menu.
	• Point at the Gadget and click the Close ☒ button on the toolbar that appears.
Change Gadget options	• Right-click on the Gadget and choose Options from the menu.
	• Point at the Gadget and click the Options 🔧 button on the toolbar that appears.

 HANDS-ON 1.3 **Add, Move, and Remove Gadgets on the Desktop**

In this exercise, you will add the Clock and Slide Show Gadgets to the Desktop. Then you will move the Gadgets before removing both from the Desktop.

Add Gadgets

1. Follow these steps to add the Clock and Slide Show Gadgets to the Desktop:

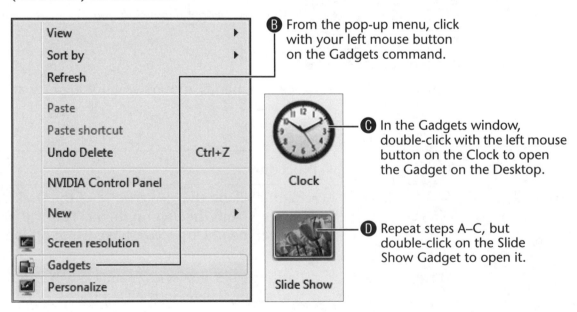

Ⓐ Point with the mouse over the background of the Desktop and click with the right (not the left) mouse button.

Ⓑ From the pop-up menu, click with your left mouse button on the Gadgets command.

Ⓒ In the Gadgets window, double-click with the left mouse button on the Clock to open the Gadget on the Desktop.

Ⓓ Repeat steps A–C, but double-click on the Slide Show Gadget to open it.

Win 7 opens the Clock and Slide Show Gadgets on the Desktop.

Move Gadgets

2. Point over the clock, hold down the left mouse button and drag the clock anywhere on the Desktop, and then release the mouse button to drop it into position.

3. Point over the slide show and then drag and drop it anywhere on the Desktop.

The clock and slide show remain where you drop them until moved again or removed from the Desktop.

Remove Gadgets

4. Point with the mouse over the clock and click with the right (not the left) mouse button.

5. From the pop-up menu, choose Close Gadget to remove it from the Desktop.

6. Point over the slide show and click the Close ⊠ button on the toolbar that appears.

Logging Off and Switching Users

Logging off the computer is different from turning the computer off. When you log off, the programs you are using are closed, your documents are saved to the hard drive, personal login information is removed from memory, and the computer is made ready for the next user to log on.

⚠ NOTE! Logging off does not shut off power to the computer. The computer is left running, but it is prepared for another user to log on.

Switch User

Multiple users can be logged on to a single computer at the same time. Each user can customize the environment of the computer to meet his or her needs. When you switch users, the previous user's information, screen settings, and programs are set aside in the computer's memory, and the new user's information is made active.

Benefits of Using Switch User   This is most useful at home when more than one person shares a computer. When each user logs on, it takes time for Win 7 to load programs and personal settings into RAM. Switching between users who have already logged on is much faster, because programs and settings already are in RAM.

QUICK REFERENCE: Logging Off and Switching Users

Task	Procedure
Log off Windows	• From the Shut Down menu ▶ button (located at the bottom of the Start menu next to the Shut Down button) choose Log Off.
Switch users	• From the Shut Down menu ▶ button, choose Switch Users. • After a pause, the screen displays available login names.
Lock and unlock Win 7	• Click the Shut Down menu ▶ button and choose Lock. This will lock the computer. • To unlock the computer, choose the icon representing the user you would like to log in as.

HANDS-ON 1.4 Practice Switch User

In this exercise, you will give the Switch User command and then log back in using your own username.

1. Follow these steps to switch users:

Ⓐ Click the Start button.

Ⓑ Click the Shut Down menu ▶ button next to the Shut Down button.

Ⓒ Choose Switch User from the menu.

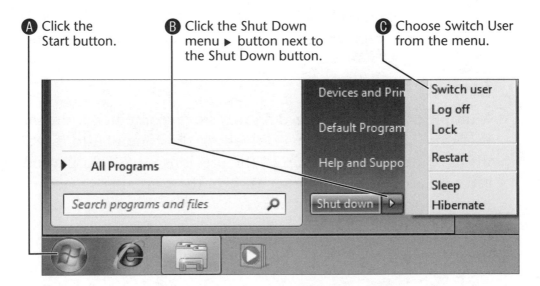

There will be a pause as Win 7 prepares to display the login screen. Wait for this screen to appear before continuing with the next step.

2. Click your username or type it in the appropriate box.

3. Type your password in the Password box and then tap the [Enter] key on the keyboard.

   After a pause, Win 7 returns you to the Desktop. You could just as easily have logged in as someone else in step 2.

Shutting Down

Win 7 is a very large collection of programs. If it is not shut down properly, you may discover upon restarting your computer that error messages appear—or worse, Win 7 doesn't start at all. Win 7 needs time to properly shut down all of its software parts and pieces correctly. Just turning off the power doesn't give Win 7 this needed time.

Shut Down Methods

There are four ways to shut down Win 7, depending on what you want to do next. Available options are displayed via the Start button using the Shut down button and the Shut down menu:

- Shut Down

- Restart

- Hibernate

- Sleep

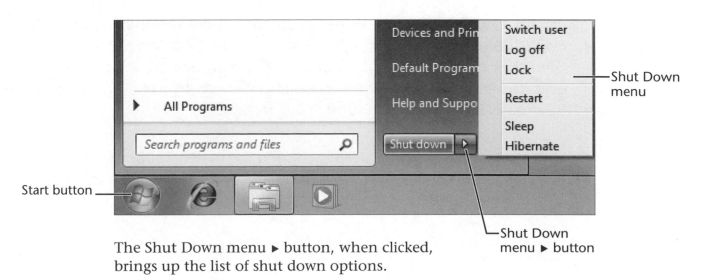

The Shut Down menu ▶ button, when clicked, brings up the list of shut down options.

Restart

The restart mode closes all open program windows, logs you out, and powers down the computer. The computer then restarts and Win 7 reloads. Sometimes Win 7 will ask you to restart the computer after a new program has been installed. The new program can't be used until the system restarts and the new software is integrated into Win 7.

Sleep

In sleep mode, the computer uses a lot less energy because the computer slows down. Any documents you are working on are saved, the processor works more slowly, the monitor is turned off, and other settings are triggered that allow the computer to save power. Most Win 7 computers also feature a sleep button on they keyboard for easy access to this command.

Most new computer keyboards feature a sleep button as a convenient means to activate the computer's sleep mode.

 TIP! On most laptops, closing the lid will immediately cause the laptop to go into sleep mode and start conserving battery power.

Hibernate

Hibernate is a more aggressive power-saving mode than sleep mode and is usually found on laptops. When a computer is put into hibernate mode, everything you were working on is saved to the hard drive. All equipment is then shut down. When the computer is turned back on, Win 7 loads everything you were working on exactly the way it was before you activated hibernate, and you can continue your work.

 TIP! If your laptop is in sleep mode and the battery drops to less than 10 percent power, Win 7 will automatically switch to hibernate so that no data is lost.

Shut Down

This command closes all programs, logs you out of the computer, and turns off the power to the computer. When you are done with the computer for the day, it is important to turn off the computer using the Shut Down command.

WARNING! Never hold down the power button to turn a computer off unless you have no other choice. Win 7 needs time to close its various parts and pieces down properly. Turning the power off abruptly can corrupt parts of the Win 7 software and can even cause the computer to not restart.

QUICK REFERENCE: Shutting Down Win 7

Task	Procedure
Shut down Win 7 and the computer	• Close all open programs. • Click the Shut Down button (located at the bottom of the Start menu). `Shut down`
Go into sleep mode	• Choose Sleep from the Shut Down menu ▸ button.
Exit sleep mode	• Move the mouse or tap the `Spacebar` on your keyboard.

HANDS-ON 1.5 Practice Using Sleep Mode

In this exercise, you will practice putting the computer into sleep mode and then back into working mode.

1. Make sure all programs are closed.

2. Follow these steps to go into sleep mode:

A Click the Start button.   **B** Click the Shut Down menu ▶ button.   **C** Choose Sleep from the menu.

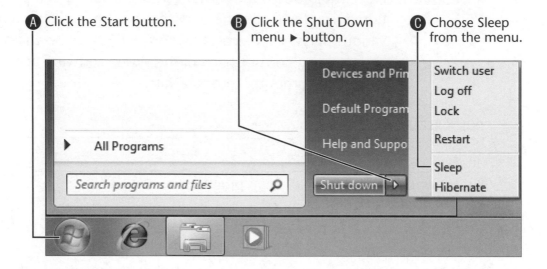

3. Move the mouse or press the Spacebar on the keyboard to bring the computer out of sleep mode.

4. If the Welcome screen appears, choose your screen name and enter your password if requested. (You may also have to use the Ctrl+Alt+Delete keys if you are in a computer lab.)

   The computer is now ready to work again.

Shut Down Win 7

Now you will end your Win 7 session by logging off.

5. Make sure any open programs are closed.

6. Click the Start ⊕ button.

7. Click the Shut Down button at the bottom of the Start menu.

   It may take the computer 15 seconds or more to completely shut down.

 Concepts Review

True/False Questions

1. Access to most features in Win 7 is through the Start button located in the bottom-left corner of the screen.   **true**   **false**   _____

2. Icons are small pictures that represent programs or other features in Win 7.   **true**   **false**   _____

3. Sleep mode is used to save energy when the computer is not going to be operated for a while.   **true**   **false**   _____

4. Drag and drop is used to move icons on the screen.   **true**   **false**   _____

5. It's okay to simply switch the power off when you're done using the computer.   **true**   **false**   _____

6. Gadgets are productivity tools designed to put information at your fingertips.   **true**   **false**   _____

Multiple Choice Questions

1. Which of these is the best password?
   Page number: _____
   a. Fido
   b. G476rty
   c. JohnSmith
   d. Password

2. Which of these is *not* a mouse action?
   Page number: _____
   a. Single-click
   b. Double-click
   c. Roll
   d. Point

3. Which item is *not* on the Shut Down menu?
   Page number: _____
   a. Switch User
   b. Restart
   c. Hibernate
   d. Pause System

4. Icons _____.
   Page number: _____
   a. are small images that can represent documents, photos, and programs
   b. can be found in many areas of Win 7, including the Desktop and the taskbar
   c. act as the start buttons for programs
   d. All of the above

Skill Builders

SKILL BUILDER 1.1 **Practice Mousing with Solitaire**

In this exercise, you will open and play Solitaire to enhance your mousing skills.

1. Click the Start ⊕ button and choose Games from the right pane.

    A new window appears to display the games that come installed with Win 7.

2. From the Games menu, double-click on the Solitaire icon. Or click once on Solitaire and tap the ⌷Enter⌷ key on the keyboard.

    A new window appears and deals the cards for a new game automatically.

3. Follow these basic mousing moves for playing Solitaire:

Click Help on the menu bar and then click View Help to learn more about Solitaire. (It's probably easiest to have a classmate show you if you don't know this game already.)

To move cards from one pile to another, drag and drop the card on its new location. (You need an ace to start placing cards in the four empty squares.)

To turn cards from the card pile over, simply click on the pile.

> **!TIP!** If the card jumps back to its original location, it was placed in an illegal location.

4. When you are finished, click Game on the menu bar and then choose New Game to start a new game of Solitaire. To close the Solitaire program, click Game on the menu bar and choose Exit.

Practice Mousing with Mousercise

In this exercise, you will practice using the mouse with the online software Mousercise.

Before You Begin: This exercise runs on the Internet, so you need to know how to navigate with a web browser. (The Internet is introduced in Lesson 6, Using the Internet.) A friend or family member should be able to help you get the exercise started in step 1 if you don't yet use the Internet.

1. Launch Internet Explorer and navigate to the web page for this book:
   `labpub.com/learn/silver/wtw7`

2. Click the Mouse Practice link for Lesson 1.

3. Follow the on-screen instructions.

4. Close ☒ the Internet Explorer window when you are finished.

Try This at Home

TRY THIS AT HOME 1.1 Practice Switch User

In this exercise, you will practice switching from one user login to another.

Before You Begin: Skip this exercise if there is only one user listed on the Win 7 Welcome screen. You need at least two user accounts to switch between users.

1. Click the Start ⊕ button.

2. Follow these steps to switch users:

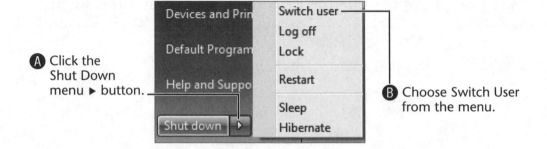

A Click the Shut Down menu ▸ button.

B Choose Switch User from the menu.

After a pause, Win 7 displays a screen with the available usernames.

3. Choose a different username that you would like to switch to, type the password, and tap the ⎵Enter⎵ key on the keyboard.

   Win 7 starts the switch. This can take 15 seconds or more to accomplish, depending on the speed of your computer and the amount of RAM available for the operation.

4. Click the Start button, click the Shut Down menu ▸ button, and choose Switch User again.

5. Log in with your own username and password.

   There is another pause as Win 7 switches you back to your Desktop. Notice that everything is just how you left it before switching to the other username.

6. Click the Start button, click the Shut Down menu ▸ button, and choose Log Off.

   There is a pause as Win 7 logs you off.

7. Log in to the other username.

8. Log off the other username.

Change a Gadget's Options

In this exercise, you will open the Clock Gadget from the list of available Gadgets and change its options.

1. Right-click on the Desktop background and choose Gadgets from the pop-up menu.

2. Double-click on the Clock Gadget from the Gadget choices presented.

3. Close ☒ the Gadget window.

4. Follow these steps to change the options for the clock:

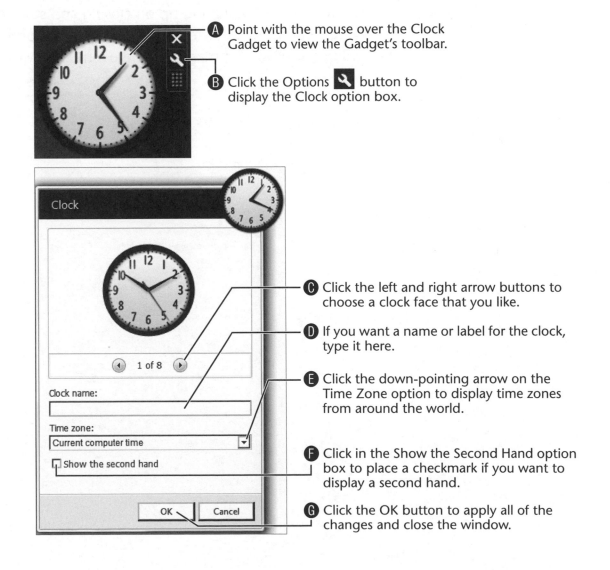

Ⓐ Point with the mouse over the Clock Gadget to view the Gadget's toolbar.

Ⓑ Click the Options 🔧 button to display the Clock option box.

Ⓒ Click the left and right arrow buttons to choose a clock face that you like.

Ⓓ If you want a name or label for the clock, type it here.

Ⓔ Click the down-pointing arrow on the Time Zone option to display time zones from around the world.

Ⓕ Click in the Show the Second Hand option box to place a checkmark if you want to display a second hand.

Ⓖ Click the OK button to apply all of the changes and close the window.

You can have more than one clock on the Desktop. You might have a different look and a different label on a second clock displaying a different time zone.

Practice Shutting Down

In this exercise, you will practice shutting down the computer properly.

1. Make sure that all of your open programs are closed.

2. From the Start menu choose Shut Down.

   The computer will take a minute or two to complete its shutdown tasks. Be patient and wait for the computer to finish.

3. If the computer doesn't turn off the power automatically, you will need to power off the computer and the monitor.

    **WARNING!** Sometimes Win 7 will hang up on closing and stop responding. Give the computer a few minutes to correct the problem before turning the power off manually and overriding Win 7.

Starting Programs

In this lesson, you will become familiar with various components of the Start menu, launch a program, learn the features used to control a program window, and begin to multitask—open and switch among multiple programs. Although applications from many different software companies are installed on your computer, the Win 7 operating system provides standardized tools for launching and controlling application programs.

LESSON OBJECTIVES

After studying this lesson, you will be able to:

- Navigate and arrange program commands on the Start menu
- Open programs from the Start menu
- Minimize, maximize, size, and move program windows
- Describe basic features of the Win 7 taskbar
- Multitask effectively using the taskbar

*Additional learning resources are available at **labpub.com/learn/silver/wtw7/***

Case Study: Starting at the Beginning

William is going back to school and has bought a new computer to help him complete his homework. He has very little experience using a computer and feels a bit confused by all of the programs. He has tried clicking on the Desktop icons and has clicked on the Start menu, but the programs have so many different purposes: Several play music, one is like a checkbook, one is for drawing pictures, another is a notepad, and there also are card games. Before learning the different applications he will be using to do his homework, he decides to first learn what the programs have in common. If he can learn the standardized Win 7 features used in most programs, it will be much easier to learn new applications. William starts with the Start menu.

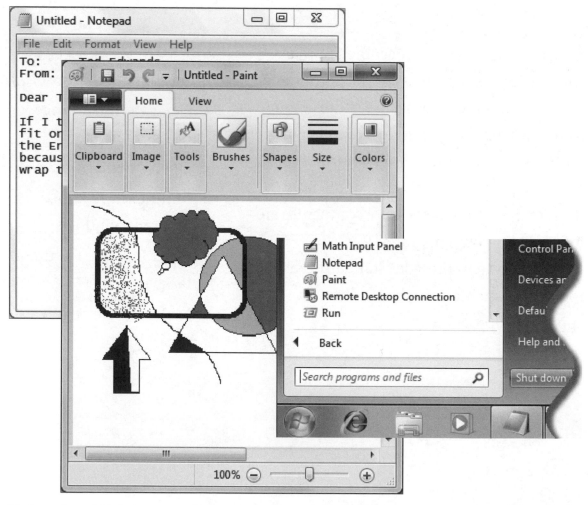

Notepad and Paint are small programs found in the Start menu's Accessories folder.

Working with the Start Menu

The Start menu is the one place you can go to launch most of the programs installed on your computer. Like all menus, the Start menu is a collection of commands. The Start button gives access to commands to launch all of the programs that come with Win 7. When you install a new program, Win 7 adds a command for it to the Start menu. Commands on a menu often have a descriptive label and an icon.

About Commands

A command is a link that can launch (start or open) a document, folder, or program, or execute a variety of other tasks. You might compare a command to a light switch on the wall used to turn on a ceiling light. Clicking (or double-clicking) on a command launches the object to which it is linked. More than one command can be linked to the same object. Commands can be located on the Desktop, in a menu, on a toolbar, or on a ribbon.

 HANDS-ON 2.1   **Display and Dismiss the Start Menu**

In this exercise, you will display and dismiss the Start menu using both the mouse and the keyboard.

1. Click the Start ⊞ button to display the Start menu.
   The Start menu is displayed. Observe the left and right panes of the Start menu.

2. Click the Start ⊞ button again to dismiss the Start menu.

3. Press the WIN ⊞ key on the keyboard to display the Start menu.

4. Press the WIN ⊞ key again to dismiss the Start menu.
   It's easy to dismiss the Start menu if you pull it up by mistake.

Start Menu Panes

The Start menu is divided into left and right panes:

- The left pane has a list of commands to various programs, including the All Programs folder. There is also a Start Search text box at the bottom.

- The right pane usually displays commands to display various parts of the computer system. At the bottom, there is also a Shut Down button with a Shut Down menu ▶ button attached.

> **!TIP!** The appearance of the Start menu may vary depending on the version of Win 7 being used on the computer. Although the appearance may vary, all Start menus function in the same manner.

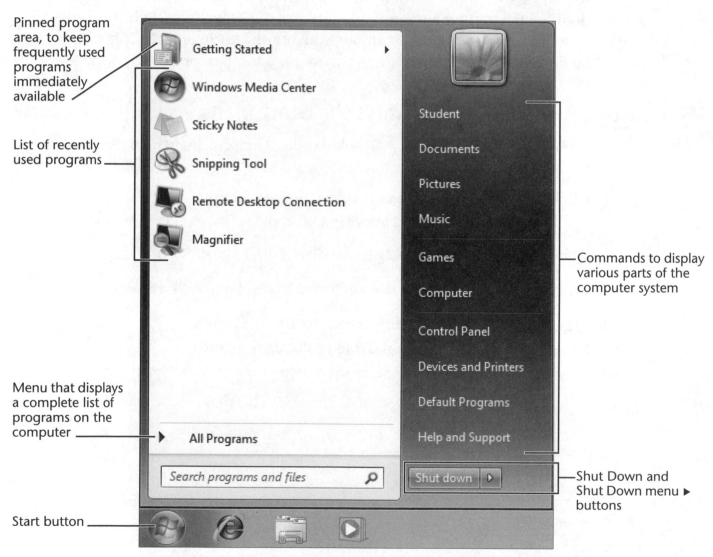

Pinned program area, to keep frequently used programs immediately available

List of recently used programs

Menu that displays a complete list of programs on the computer

Commands to display various parts of the computer system

Shut Down and Shut Down menu ▶ buttons

Start button

Major features of the Start menu

Jump Lists in the Start Menu

A new feature in Win 7 is the use of Jump Lists in Start menu. Jump Lists are attached to Start menu commands and provide additional commands that link to files recently created with that program or that link to other related tasks. When a Jump List is attached to a command in the Start menu, a right-pointing arrow ► can be seen on the right side of the command. The list will "fly out" to the right for viewing when the mouse pointer is placed over the command.

A right-pointing arrow on the Start menu command indicates that there is an attached Jump List.

Launching Programs

Commands in the left pane of the Start menu are divided into three sections with gray menu separators:

- The top section has commands that are "pinned" in placed until removed by you.

- The center section has a list of recently used programs. Win 7 adds commands to this list as you launch new programs.

- The All Programs command near the bottom of the Start menu displays a list of most programs installed on the computer. Win 7 adds a command to this list automatically when a program is first installed.

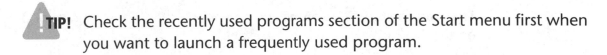

!TIP! Check the recently used programs section of the Start menu first when you want to launch a frequently used program.

HANDS-ON 2.2 **Launch a Program from the Start Menu**

In this exercise, you will launch the Paint program from the Start menu.

1. Use your mouse or the keyboard to display the Start menu.

Run your mouse pointer over the commands in the left pane and notice the selection bar that appears when your mouse pointer is above a command. You can click anywhere along the selection bar to launch a command.

2. Click the All Programs command.

3. Follow these steps to start the Paint program:

Ⓐ Drag the scroll box (in the middle of the scroll bar) downward if necessary until you see a folder labeled Accessories.

Ⓑ Click the Accessories folder to open it.

Ⓒ Click the Paint command to launch the program.

Windows DVD Maker	
Windows Fax and Scan	Student
Windows Media Center	
Windows Media Player	Documents
Windows Update	
XPS Viewer	Pictures
Accessories	
Calculator	Music
Command Prompt	
Connect to a Network Projector	Games
Connect to a Projector	
Getting Started	Computer
Math Input Panel	
Notepad	
Paint	

The Start menu will be dismissed, and after a short pause, the Paint program will open on the Desktop.

⚠️**TIP!** In the rest of this book, Start menu commands will be written like this: Choose Start→All Programs→Accessories→Paint.

4. Close the Paint program by clicking the red Close button in the upper-right corner of the window.

Recently Used Programs List

Win 7 automatically adds commands for programs to the recently used programs list of the Start menu. Sometimes a program is added to the list the first time you launch it. Other times you may need to use a program twice to have it added to the list. When the recently used programs list becomes full, the command of the program that has been unused the longest is hidden. You can also remove a command from the recently used program list.

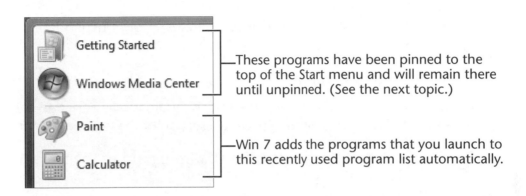

These programs have been pinned to the top of the Start menu and will remain there until unpinned. (See the next topic.)

Win 7 adds the programs that you launch to this recently used program list automatically.

Pinning Programs to the Start Menu

Commands can be pinned to the top section of the left pane and stay there until unpinned. Unlike the recently used program list, pinned commands are not added or hidden by Win 7; *you* choose which programs get pinned or unpinned.

 TIP! Go ahead and pin programs you use a lot. This leaves more room on the frequently used programs list for programs you use less often.

QUICK REFERENCE: Pinning Commands to the Start Menu

Task	Procedure
Remove a program from the recently used programs list	*Right*-click (not left-click) any program command in the Start menu and choose Remove from This List from the pop-up menu.
Pin a command to the Start menu	*Right*-click any program command in the Start menu and choose Pin to Start Menu from the pop-up menu, or drag the command from the recently used programs list and drop it in the pinned section.
Unpin a Start menu command	*Right*-click on the pinned command and choose Unpin from Start Menu from the pop-up menu.

HANDS-ON 2.3 **Pin Commands to the Start Menu**

In this exercise, you will open and close a program from the All Programs folder. A command will be added to the recently used programs list. You will then pin commands to the top section of the Start menu and, finally, unpin the commands from the top of the Start menu.

1. Choose Start 🌐 →All Programs→Accessories→Notepad.

Win 7 launches the Notepad program, a very basic text-typing program.

2. Close Notepad by clicking the red Close ▨ X button in the upper-right corner of the window.

3. Click the Start 🌐 button.

Notice that a Notepad command has been automatically added to the recently used programs list in the center section of the left pane.

4. Follow these steps to pin the Notepad program to the Start menu:

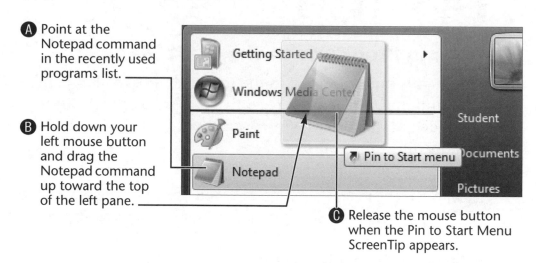

Ⓐ Point at the Notepad command in the recently used programs list.

Ⓑ Hold down your left mouse button and drag the Notepad command up toward the top of the left pane.

Ⓒ Release the mouse button when the Pin to Start Menu ScreenTip appears.

Win 7 places the Notepad command into the pinned list.

5. Click a clear area of the Desktop to close the Start menu.

6. Click the Start 🌐 button.

The Notepad program appears right where you pinned it.

Pin Another Program

7. Follow these steps to pin another program to the Start menu:

Ⓐ Click All Programs to display the program list.

Ⓑ Click the Accessories folder.

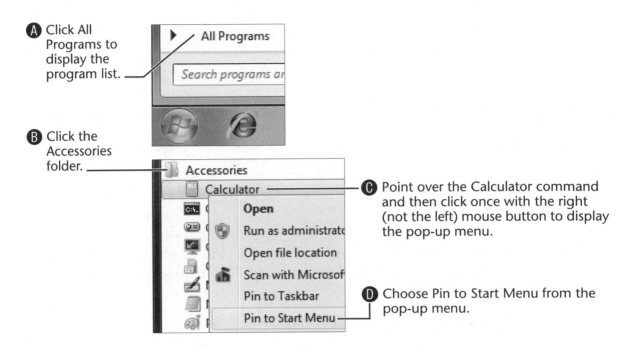

Ⓒ Point over the Calculator command and then click once with the right (not the left) mouse button to display the pop-up menu.

Ⓓ Choose Pin to Start Menu from the pop-up menu.

Win 7 pins the program command to the bottom of the pinned program list.

8. Click a clear area of the Desktop to close the Start menu and then click the Start ⊞ button again.

Unpin the Programs

To clear the pinned programs for the next student, you will unpin the two programs.

9. Follow these steps to unpin the Calculator command:

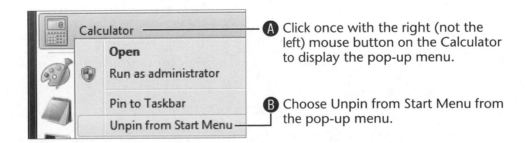

Ⓐ Click once with the right (not the left) mouse button on the Calculator to display the pop-up menu.

Ⓑ Choose Unpin from Start Menu from the pop-up menu.

Win 7 removes the command from the pinned area.

10. Right-click the Notepad command in the pinned area and then choose Unpin from Start Menu from the pop-up menu.

11. Click a clear area of the Desktop to close the Start menu.

Controlling Program Windows

Every program you open in Win 7 is displayed within its own window. This window, known as the program window, has controls and features that are similar in most programs. These basic controls are Win 7 standards; learn to use them in one program, and you will be able to work with similar controls in most new programs you use.

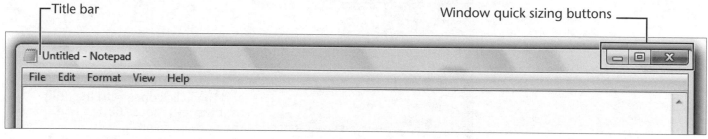

Title bar

Window quick sizing buttons

Untitled - Notepad

File   Edit   Format   View   Help

Here is an example of a program window for Notepad, a program that comes with Win 7. The quick sizing buttons and title bar are standard controls in all program windows.

Quick Sizing Buttons

The quick sizing buttons consist of the Minimize, Maximize, Restore Down, and Close buttons located in the upper-right corner of most program windows. These buttons, along with the program button on the taskbar, are used to reconfigure or to close a program window.

QUICK REFERENCE: Using Window Quick Sizing Buttons

Button	Name	How It Works
	Minimize	Removes the program window from the screen but continues to run it and leaves its program button on the taskbar
	Maximize	Enlarges a program window to fill the screen
	Restore Down	Resizes a program window to the smaller size it was before it was last maximized
	Close	Exits a program
	Program button (on taskbar)	Minimizes an open window or reopens a window that has been minimized

The Minimize and Maximize Buttons   The Minimize button shrinks the program window from the Desktop, leaving only its program button on the taskbar. The program continues to run. To open the program window again, click the program's button on the taskbar. The program will open again to the size it was before it was minimized.

!TIP! If a program window is open, you also can click its program button on the taskbar to minimize the window.

Maximize is just the opposite of minimize. Maximize enlarges a program to fill the entire Desktop so that other programs become hidden behind it.

Why minimize or maximize programs? Having multiple programs open on your Desktop can be like having a messy desk. Minimizing windows will hide the distracting clutter of open windows, while maximizing a window will simply cover other opened windows.

Minimize Compared to Close   The Minimize button makes a program window shrink from the screen, but it does not close the program. If you are in the middle of a Spider Solitaire game and minimize, the Spider Solitaire program button is still on the taskbar. When you click the program's taskbar button, the game will return to its previous size, and your card game is ready for you to continue.

When you click the Close button, you end the card game and exit the program, and the program button is removed from the taskbar.

FROM THE KEYBOARD
_____

Alt + F4 to close (exit) a program
_____

!TIP! A quick way to close a minimized program is to *right*-click the program button on the taskbar. This displays the control menu (shown in the figure to the right) that includes a Close Window command at the bottom.

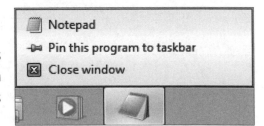

The Maximize and Restore Down Buttons The center quick sizing button toggles between the Maximize and Restore Down buttons; they are never shown at the same time. If you click Maximize, the center button changes to Restore Down. Conversely, if you click Restore Down, the center button changes to Maximize, as shown here:

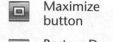

Maximize button

Restore Down button

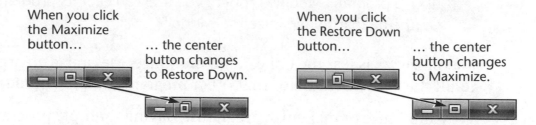

When you click the Maximize button...

... the center button changes to Restore Down.

When you click the Restore Down button...

... the center button changes to Maximize.

The Program Button on the Taskbar When a program is opened, its program button appears on the taskbar. The button displays the program's icon without a label. If you position the mouse cursor over the program button (without

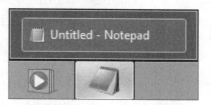

clicking), additional information about the program will be displayed on a ScreenTip. Clicking on the program button can minimize an open program window, restore a minimized window to its former size, or make an inactive program active.

Quick Sizing Button Exceptions Occasionally a program will not use all of the standard controls. Certain control buttons may be missing or *grayed out*. This is discussed later in the Hands-On section of this lesson, but in the following example, the Minimize and Maximize buttons are missing:

The Aero theme was used for images in this book. The appearance of quick sizing buttons may change with other themes or in different programs, but their functions remain the same. Following are some variations.

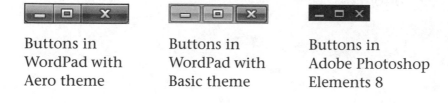

Buttons in WordPad with Aero theme

Buttons in WordPad with Basic theme

Buttons in Adobe Photoshop Elements 8

HANDS-ON 2.4 **Practice Using Quick Sizing Buttons**

In this exercise, you will open the Paint program and practice using the quick sizing buttons to minimize, maximize, and restore down the program window.

1. Choose Start →All Programs→Accessories→Paint to launch the program. (If necessary, review steps 1–3 in Hands-On 2.2.)

    The Paint program will open either maximized or in a restored-down size.

2. If the program window does not fill the screen, click the Maximize ▣ button.

    The program window enlarges to fill the entire Desktop (except for the taskbar). Also notice that the center quick sizing button has changed to a Restore Down button.

    It is usually a good idea to maximize ▣ any program window when it first opens to take full advantage of the entire screen.

3. Click the Restore Down ▣ button.

    Notice how the program window is restored back to its original smaller size.

4. Click the Minimize ▬ button.

    Now you can see the Desktop. The program window shrinks off of the Desktop, leaving only a program button on the taskbar. Locate the button for the Paint program on the taskbar at the bottom of the screen.

5. Click the Paint program button on the taskbar to restore the Paint program onto your Desktop.

Program button on the taskbar

Each program button on the taskbar has an icon that helps you to identify the program. Paint uses a paint palette and a brush as its icon.

6. Click the Close ▬x▬ button to exit Paint.

Moving and Resizing Program Windows

Program windows can be moved around on the Desktop the way you move papers and objects around your desk at home. Unlike your desk at home, program windows can be resized to fill the Desktop or reduced to a smaller size.

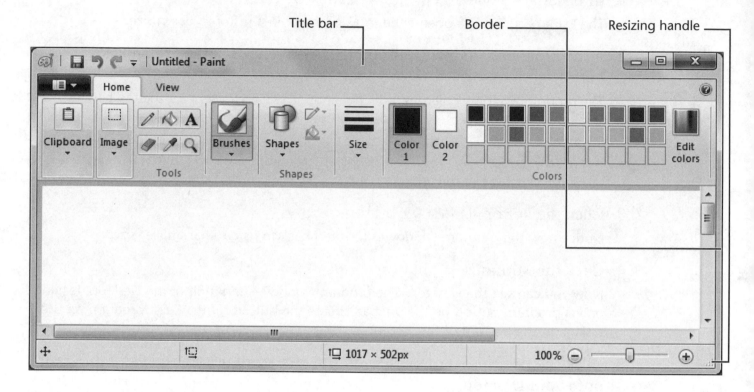

Title bar ____ Border ____ Resizing handle ____

Title Bar   The title bar on top of every program window serves several purposes. It displays the name of the program, and it also may display the name of the document or other object being edited by that program. Control buttons are located at the right and left ends of the bar.

Finally, the title bar provides a *handle* to move the program window. If you position the tip of your mouse pointer over any empty space on its title bar (not its border), you can hold down your left mouse button and drag a program window around the Desktop.

Resizing a Window   To resize a restored-down program window, position the mouse pointer over the resizing handle, located in the bottom-right corner. When the mouse pointer changes into a double-headed arrow, you can hold down your left mouse button and drag to resize.

A program window has a narrow border surrounding it. You can also resize a window by dragging the border from any side or any corner. Dragging any side border will resize only that side of the window. Dragging any corner will resize both sides attached to the corner.

If your mouse pointer will not change to a double-headed arrow when you point at a border, then the program window cannot be resized.

Resizable

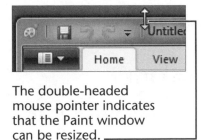

Not resizable

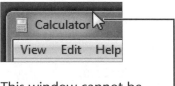

The double-headed mouse pointer indicates that the Paint window can be resized.

This window cannot be resized because the mouse pointer did not change when pointed at a border.

!TIP! New users will find the resizing handle in the lower-right corner easier to use than the narrow border because the handle has a larger "hot spot."

The Snap Feature   Another new feature in Win 7 is called Snap. Snap is a new way to maximize, restore down, or view two windows side-by-side on the Desktop. Snap is accomplished by simply dragging windows to the top or sides of the Desktop.

QUICK REFERENCE: Using Snap to Resize Windows

Task	Procedure
Maximize a window	• Use the title bar to drag a restored-down window to the top edge of the Desktop until the mouse pointer touches.
Restore down a window	• Use the title bar to drag a maximized window away from the top edge of the Desktop.
Display two windows side-by-side	• Use the title bar to drag one window to the left edge of the Desktop until the mouse pointer touches. The window fills the left half of the Desktop. • Use the title bar to drag another window to the right edge of the Desktop until the mouse pointer touches. The window fills the right half of the Desktop.

HANDS-ON 2.5 **Move, Resize, and Snap a Window**

In this exercise, you will move, resize, and snap the Paint program window.

1. Choose Start 🪟→All Programs→Accessories→Paint to launch the program. (If necessary, review steps 1–3 in Hands-On 2.1.)

2. If necessary, restore down the program window.

3. Use the title bar to move the program window around the Desktop.

⚠️**TIP!** A program window cannot be resized if it is maximized.

4. Practice resizing the program window using the resizing handle and border sides or corners.

5. Initiate the Snap feature by using the title bar to drag the window to the left edge of the Desktop until the mouse pointer touches the edge.

6. Repeat step 5 by dragging the window to the right edge, bottom edge, and top edge, and finally by dragging the window away from all edges.

7. Close ▬ **x** ▬ the Paint program.

Nonstandard Program Windows

Although Win 7 establishes *standards* used by most programs, there are times when the standards are ignored or modified for appearance reasons or because certain functions are not necessary to use a program. In some programs the features are simply missing, while in other programs the features are modified in appearance or grayed out and do not work.

HANDS-ON 2.6 **Open Sticky Notes and the Calculator**

In this exercise, you will open Sticky Notes and the Calculator to discover some of their nonstandard features.

Open Sticky Notes

1. Choose Start 🪟→Sticky Notes.

2. Follow these steps to explore the few features available on a Sticky Note:

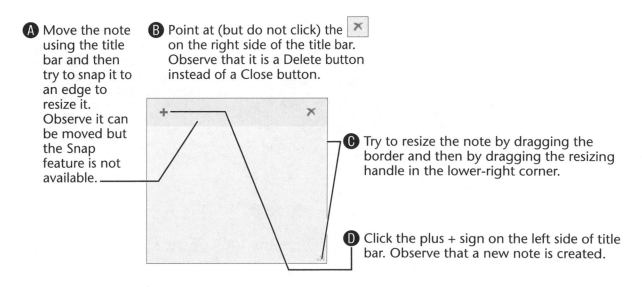

A Move the note using the title bar and then try to snap it to an edge to resize it. Observe it can be moved but the Snap feature is not available.

B Point at (but do not click) the ☒ on the right side of the title bar. Observe that it is a Delete button instead of a Close button.

C Try to resize the note by dragging the border and then by dragging the resizing handle in the lower-right corner.

D Click the plus + sign on the left side of title bar. Observe that a new note is created.

Open Calculator

3. Choose Start 🪟→All Programs→Accessories→Calculator to launch the program.

4. Follow these steps to try out some features of the program:

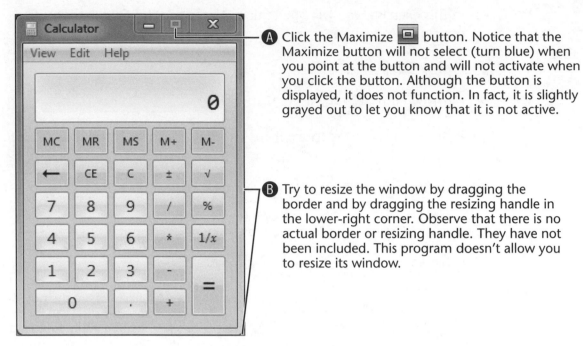

Calculator's Standard View

A Click the Maximize [▢] button. Notice that the Maximize button will not select (turn blue) when you point at the button and will not activate when you click the button. Although the button is displayed, it does not function. In fact, it is slightly grayed out to let you know that it is not active.

B Try to resize the window by dragging the border and by dragging the resizing handle in the lower-right corner. Observe that there is no actual border or resizing handle. They have not been included. This program doesn't allow you to resize its window.

5. Follow these steps to change the look of the Calculator window:

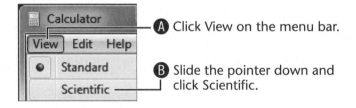

A Click View on the menu bar.

B Slide the pointer down and click Scientific.

⚠️ **NOTE!** In future exercises, this type of menu bar command will be written like this: Choose View→Scientific from the menu bar.

This is the way to expand the Calculator's program window and change its function to a scientific calculator, with many more features.

6. Close ⬛ the Calculator program and click the Delete Note ⊠ button to remove any Sticky Notes.

Working with the Win 7 Taskbar

The taskbar runs the width of the Desktop at the bottom of the screen. The center section of the taskbar displays the programs you have opened. When a program is opened, its program button is placed on the taskbar.

Only one program window can be *active,* and it will be displayed in front of other inactive programs open on your Desktop. The active program button will be brighter than other program buttons on the taskbar. Clicking on an inactive program button will make that program active and move its window in front of others on the Desktop.

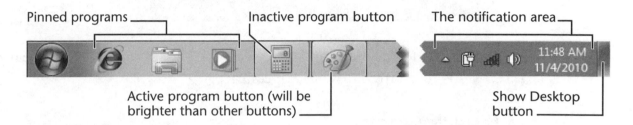

Pinned programs — Inactive program button — The notification area —

Active program button (will be brighter than other buttons) — Show Desktop button —

Notification Area

The Notification Area on the right end of the taskbar has four primary functions in Win 7:

- Display the system clock and current date

- Display icons for tasks and functions that are running in the background, such as antivirus software

- Display notifications of system events, such as program updates

- Provide access to some programs whose icons display there

Icon ScreenTips Your computer can have many icons in the Notification Area. It can be difficult to determine their purpose or even to which program they are linked. When you point with the mouse over an icon, a ScreenTip appears to describe the name of the program linked to the icon and other information about it.

ScreenTips can tell you about each icon in the Notification Area.

HANDS-ON 2.7 Change Taskbar Settings

In this exercise, you will open the taskbar and Start Menu Properties dialog box to observe setting options and to make changes to the taskbar settings.

1. Follow these steps to display the taskbar properties window:

A Right-click a clear portion of the taskbar to display its pop-up menu.

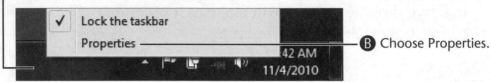

B Choose Properties.

2. When the Taskbar and Start Menu Properties dialog box appears, follow these steps to change taskbar appearance:

A Click the Taskbar tab.

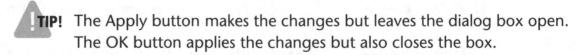

B Click once (do not double-click) on the Use small icons option box. (The box should have a checkmark before you go on to step C.)

C Click the Apply (not OK) button near the bottom of the dialog box to display smaller icons on the taskbar.

The icons are smaller, which enables more program buttons to be displayed on the taskbar. However, notice that the current date is no longer displayed in the Notification Area.

⚠ TIP! The Apply button makes the changes but leaves the dialog box open. The OK button applies the changes but also closes the box.

3. Remove the checkmark in the Use Small Icons option box and click Apply again.

Notice that larger icons have been restored on the taskbar.

4. Click OK to close the dialog box.

Pinning and Unpinning Programs

Win 7 enables users to pin program buttons to the taskbar in much the same way they pin programs to the Start menu. Typically, the taskbar is set to be displayed even when windows are maximized, which means that the pinned program buttons are always available. A pinned program that is not currently open will not have a button border around the icon.

Pinned program buttons do not have borders when the program is closed.

QUICK REFERENCE: Pinning and Unpinning Programs

Task	Procedure
Pin a program	• *Right*-click on the program button to display pop-up menu.
	• Choose Pin This Program to Taskbar.
	• The program button will remain on the taskbar even when the program is closed until it is unpinned.
Unpin a program	• *Right*-click on the program button to display pop-up menu.
	• Choose Unpin This Program from Taskbar.

HANDS-ON 2.8 **Pin and Unpin a Program**

In this exercise, you will open Notepad, pin the program button to the taskbar, and then unpin the program from the taskbar.

1. Choose Start 🟦 →All Programs→Accessories→Notepad to launch the program.

2. Follow these step to pin the program to the taskbar:

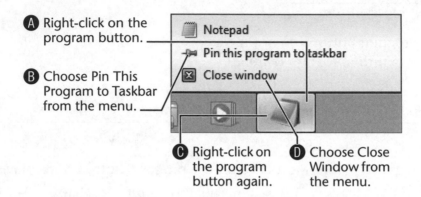

(A) Right-click on the program button.

(B) Choose Pin This Program to Taskbar from the menu.

(C) Right-click on the program button again.

(D) Choose Close Window from the menu.

The Notepad icon remains on the taskbar. Once the program is closed, it no longer has a button border around it.

3. Follow these steps to unpin the Notepad program:

(A) Right-click on the program button.

(B) Choose Unpin This Program from Taskbar from the menu.

The Notepad icon is removed from the taskbar.

Multitasking

One useful feature of Win 7 is its ability to *multitask*. Multitasking enables the computer to run multiple programs or operations at the same time. Multitasking lets Win 7 run various tasks and activities in the background that you might not even be aware of, such as downloading software patches, monitoring the security of your computer, and performing hundreds of other small tasks. You also can take advantage of multitasking to help you to become more efficient with your time in front of the computer. You can have several programs open, be printing a document, and be listening to a music CD—all at the same time.

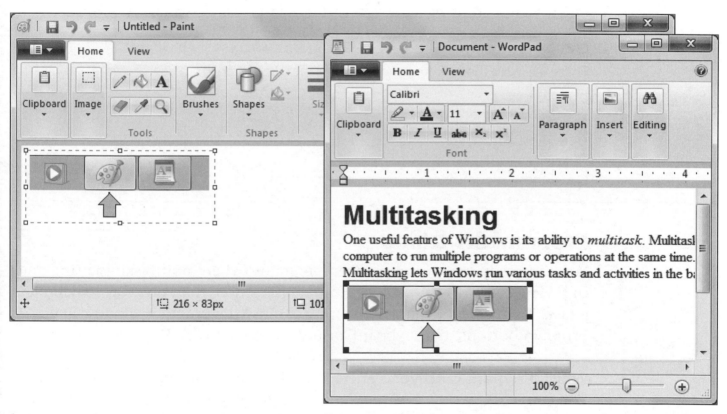

Multitasking lets you perform many tasks simultaneously: check email, pay bills online, listen to music, and print documents.

HANDS-ON 2.9 Open Multiple Programs

In this exercise, you will open three programs from the Start menu (found in the Accessories folder of All Programs) and watch the program buttons be added to the taskbar.

1. Click the Start ⊕ button to display the Start menu.

   Review the commands in the recently used programs list in the left pane.

2. Click Calculator if available in the left pane or choose All Programs→Accessories→Calculator.

   Observe the program button added to the taskbar with the program logo and name.

3. Open WordPad using Start ⊕→All Programs→Accessories→WordPad.

4. Open Paint using Start ⊕→All Programs→Accessories→Paint.

   There are now three program buttons on the taskbar, one for each program.

Leave these programs open for the next exercise.

Program Switching

You can easily switch among open programs (when multitasking) using one of several switching tools. Win 7 often offers more than one way to complete a task. To make a program active, you can use the program window, the program buttons, the keyboard, or the Switch Between Windows button.

Which Program Is Active?   There is a rule when running multiple programs: You can work in only one program at a time. If you think of open program windows like objects on your desk, the object you are currently using would be the active object and would, most likely, be on top of the other objects.

Win 7 places the active program window in front (on top) of the inactive windows. The Close button for the active program is red, the borders are bluer, and its program button on the taskbar is brighter. Inactive windows have a grayed-out Close button and grayed-out borders, and the color of inactive program buttons is darker.

Inactive buttons are darker in color.

The active program button is brighter.

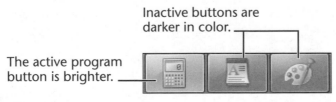

HANDS-ON 2.10 **Switch Programs**

In this exercise, you will change the active program window by clicking on inactive program windows and by clicking on inactive program buttons located on the taskbar.

Before You Begin: Three programs (Calculator, WordPad, and Paint) from Hands-On 2.9 should be opened on the Desktop.

1. Follow these steps to make Calculator the active program:

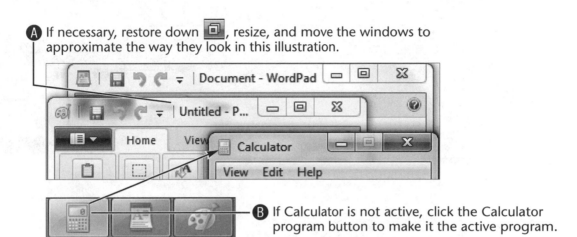

A If necessary, restore down [⧉], resize, and move the windows to approximate the way they look in this illustration.

B If Calculator is not active, click the Calculator program button to make it the active program.

2. Follow these steps to change the active program:

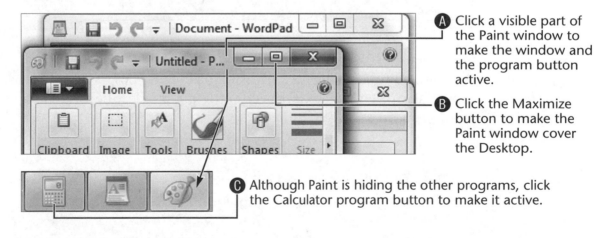

A Click a visible part of the Paint window to make the window and the program button active.

B Click the Maximize button to make the Paint window cover the Desktop.

C Although Paint is hiding the other programs, click the Calculator program button to make it active.

If any part of an inactive window can be seen, clicking the window will make it active, but avoid clicking its Close button! If windows are maximized, use the program button to make other programs active.

3. Make WordPad active and close [✕] the program.
Leave Calculator and Paint open.

The Flip Command

The Flip command enables you to quickly switch or "flip" between open programs. You access the command using the keyboard.

FROM THE KEYBOARD

Alt + Tab to switch between opened programs

Flip with Aero interface

Flip with normal interface

The Flip command displays icons for each open program window and the Desktop. The selected (boxed) program window becomes active when you finish the command.

 TIP! The Flip command is the quickest way to switch between open programs while keeping your hands on the keyboard.

HANDS-ON 2.11 **Flip Between Active Programs**

In this exercise, you will flip (switch) between Calculator, Paint, and the Desktop.

1. Make Paint the active program if it is inactive.

2. Hold down the ⌐Alt⌐ key on the keyboard and keep it held down until step 5. (Use your left thumb so you can tap the ⌐Tab⌐ key in the next step.)

3. Tap the ⌐Tab⌐ key once (while continuing to hold down ⌐Alt⌐ key).

   The Task Switcher box appears. The order of the icons for open programs can be different and will change depending on which program was active when you gave the flip command. The Desktop icon will always be on the right.

4. While holding down the ⌐Alt⌐ key, tap the ⌐Tab⌐ key until Calculator is chosen in the Task Switcher window, as shown here.

5. Release the ⌐Alt⌐ key.

   The Calculator program becomes active and jumps to the front of the Desktop.

6. Practice using ⌐Alt⌐+⌐Tab⌐ to switch among programs and the Desktop.

   Leave Calculator and Paint open.

Aero 3D Flip   3D Flip is a way to flip through open programs and the Desktop. This feature is found only on versions of Win 7 with the Aero interface. 3D Flip is launched using the [Ctrl]+WIN+[Tab] keys. See the Switching Between Programs with Flip and 3D Flip Quick Reference table below.

FROM THE KEYBOARD

[Ctrl]+ +[Tab] to launch 3D Flip

When 3D Flip is launched, regular program windows are minimized and replaced with semitransparent, three-dimensional program windows arranged like flip cards in a revolving file. 3D Flip shows current activity in the program windows. If a movie is playing in an opened program, you will see it playing in the 3D Flip window.

 Some computer labs do not support the Aero interface. You can see an example on the web page for this book.

QUICK REFERENCE: Switching Programs with Flip and 3D Flip

Task	Procedure
Use the Flip command	• Hold down the [Alt] key and then tap the [Tab] key to display the Flip window.
	• While continuing to hold down the [Alt] key, keep tapping the [Tab] key until the icon for the program you want to use is selected.
	• Release the [Alt] key. The program window you choose is now active.
Use the 3D Flip command	NOTE: This command works only on computers equipped to run the Aero interface.
	• Hold down the [Ctrl] key and the ▦ key and then press the [Tab] key.
	• Use the cursor (arrow) keys [←] and [→] to move the various program windows to the front of the stack.
	• Click once on the desired program window. (It does not have to be on the top.)

Show Desktop, Aero Peek, and Aero Shake

Win 7 has provided other features to deal with multiple windows in quick and efficient ways:

Show Desktop Button—The Show Desktop button is located at the far right end of the taskbar. The purpose of Show Desktop is to help you quickly clear the Desktop of window clutter. Instead of minimizing one window at a time, you can minimize all windows at the same time.

The Show Desktop button is located at the right end of the taskbar.

Aero Peek—Aero Peek is a new feature in the Aero versions of Win 7 that lets you see the entire Desktop "through" the open windows by temporarily making them transparent.

Aero Shake—Aero Shake is a new Aero feature that lets you quickly minimize all but one open window.

QUICK REFERENCE: Using Aero Peek, Show Desktop, and Aero Shake

Task	Procedure
Use Aero Peek to make all windows transparent	• Hover the mouse pointer over the Show Desktop button and all windows become transparent. Note: This feature is available only in Aero versions of Win 7.
Use Show Desktop to minimize all windows	• If there are any open windows on the Desktop, click the Show Desktop button.
Restore all minimized windows	• If all windows are minimized, click the Show Desktop button.
Use Aero Shake to minimize all but one window	• Point at the title bar of the window you do not want to minimize. • Hold down the left mouse button and "shake" the window by dragging back and forth quickly.

HANDS-ON 2.12 **Use Aero Peek, Show Desktop, and Aero Shake**

In this exercise, you will use the Show Desktop button and practice Peek and Shake to change the open programs. Peek and Shake require Aero to be available and turned on.

Before You Begin: Calculator and Paint programs from Hands-On 2.11 should be opened on the Desktop

Use Aero Peek

1. Hover (do not click) the mouse pointer over the Show Desktop button and then move it away from the button.

   Notice that all windows become transparent with only window borders showing, enabling you to see the Desktop behind.

Use Show Desktop

2. Click the Show Desktop button to minimize all open windows.

3. Click the Show Desktop button again to restore the windows back to their previous sizes.

Use Aero Shake

4. Point at the title bar of a window and "shake" it by dragging the window back and forth quickly.

   Notice that the other window minimizes, leaving the shaken window the active window.

5. Shake the active window again to restore the minimized window.

6. Close ▃ X ▃ all windows.

The Usefulness of Multitasking

Multitasking—the ability to run more than one task at a time—is a powerful tool. Coupled with today's sophisticated processors and Win 7's new features, multitasking can make your work time more efficient and your personal time more fun.

Before the advent of Microsoft Windows, PCs could run only one program at a time. If you were printing a long document from an older PC, you had to wait to check your email or to continue playing Solitaire. One task had to be finished before you could carry out another task.

The first version of Windows gave us the ability to multitask. Win 7 has increased multitasking capabilities, enabling a multitude of processes to run in the background, such as antivirus protection, the Clock Gadget, and instant messaging. At the same time, you can be printing a document, downloading a movie from the Internet, catching up on your email, and listening to music. These tasks no longer have to be done one at a time.

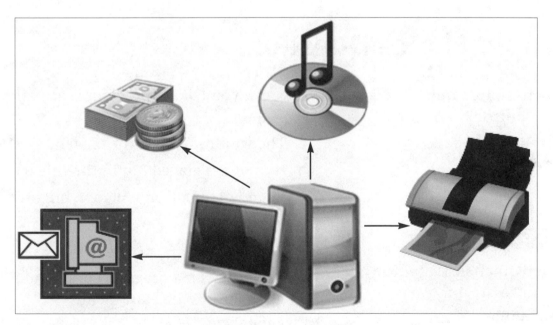

Multitasking lets you perform many tasks simultaneously: check email, pay bills online, listen to music, and print documents.

Concepts Review

True/False Questions

1. Program commands are automatically added to the Start menu when programs are installed on the computer.   **true**   **false** _____

2. Program commands in the Start menu are like light switches to launch programs.   **true**   **false** _____

3. A Jump List can provide quick access to recently used files.   **true**   **false** _____

4. If you open three programs, you will have three active program windows.   **true**   **false** _____

5. Aero 3D Flip is not available on all versions of Win 7.   **true**   **false** _____

6. Using Minimize, Maximize, and Restore Down to resize a window is called multitasking.   **true**   **false** _____

Multiple Choice Questions

1. Which is not a quick sizing button?

   Page number: _____
   a. ▣
   b. ▣
   c. ▶
   d. ✕

2. Which quick sizing button minimizes a window?

   Page number: _____
   a. ✕
   b. ▬
   c. ▶
   d. ▣

3. How can you tell if a program is active?

   Page number: _____
   a. The window will be the biggest.
   b. Its name is grayed out in the title bar.
   c. Its program button will look brighter on the Win 7 taskbar.
   d. All of the above

4. What happens if a program command is in the pinned program area of the Start menu?

   Page number: _____
   a. It stays until the computer is shut down.
   b. The program command is locked until it is unpinned.
   c. The program launches when the computer is started.
   d. It stays there until it is unpinned.

Skill Builders

SKILL BUILDER 2.1   Pin and Unpin Programs

In this exercise, you will pin two commands to the Start menu and use the commands to launch both programs. Finally, you will unpin the commands from the Start menu.

Add Two Programs to the Pinned List

1. Choose Start ⊞ →All Programs→Accessories.

2. Right-click the WordPad and Paint items to pin these commands to the pinned programs area of the Start menu.

3. Click the Back command to close All Programs as shown at right.

   The Back command closes the All Programs folder, so you can view the recently used and pinned programs lists. Notice that the newly pinned programs are on the pinned list.

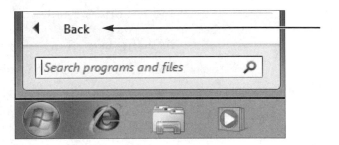

Launch Pinned Programs

4. Click WordPad to launch the program.

5. Launch Paint using Start ⊞ →Paint.

   Leave the programs open on the Desktop for the next exercise.

Remove the New Commands

6. Open the Start ⊞ menu.

7. Right-click WordPad and Paint and unpin them from the pinned list.

SKILL BUILDER 2.2 Practice Multitasking

In this exercise, you will practice multitasking by using the control features discussed in this lesson.

Before You Begin: WordPad and Paint should be open from Skill Builder 2.1.

1. Click the WordPad program button on the taskbar to make it active.

   WordPad jumps in front of the other window, and its title bar changes to show it is the active program. Also notice that WordPad's taskbar button appears brighter than the other program's button.

2. Click the Paint program button on the taskbar to make it active.

3. Maximize  the Paint window.

   Let's say that you wanted to make WordPad the active program again. Because WordPad is hidden under Paint, you need to use its taskbar button to make the program active.

4. Click the WordPad program button on the taskbar to make WordPad active.

   WordPad pops above the Paint window, ready for you to type.

5. Restore down ▣ each program.

   Each program now has a window size that partially fills the Desktop.

6. Practice resizing and moving each program window.

7. Minimize both programs at the same time using the Show Desktop button at the right end of the taskbar, as shown at right.

   The purpose of the Show Desktop button at the right end of the taskbar is to minimize all open programs with a single click, giving you quick access to the Desktop.

8. Follow the steps to the right to quickly close the minimized WordPad program.

9. Use the same right-click method on the Paint taskbar button to close its window.

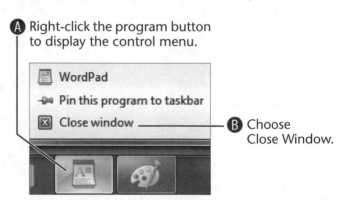

Ⓐ Right-click the program button to display the control menu.

Ⓑ Choose Close Window.

Working with a Program

In this lesson, you will explore two programs that come with Win 7: a picture-editing program called Paint and a word-processing program called WordPad. As you use these programs that have very different purposes, you will learn similarities and differences between their program controls, including menus, toolbars, ribbons, mouse pointers, and scroll bars. You also will learn widely used computer skills and program concepts, including typing and editing text on a computer; cutting, copying, and pasting text and pictures; and saving your creations on the computer's internal hard drive or on other storage devices such as a USB flash drive. Keep in mind as you work through this lesson that some of the skills and features are unique to these programs, but many are part of the standard features found in other Win 7 programs.

LESSON OBJECTIVES

After studying this lesson, you will be able to:

- Use common features found in drop-down menus, on toolbars and ribbons, and on the scroll bars

- Use the mouse effectively as the appearance and function of the mouse pointer changes

- Type and edit text in a computer program

- Cut or copy text or pictures and then paste them into another location

- Save files or copies of files on the internal hard drive or on a USB flash drive

Additional learning resources are available at labpub.com/learn/silver/wtw7/

Case Study: Creating a Letter and a Map

Sylvia wants to start a small home-based business. Her hobby for years has been raising goldfish. She thinks there is an untapped market in her area for setting up small aquariums in offices and providing aquarium maintenance services. To test the market, Sylvia wants to send letters and deliver fliers to local businesses explaining the products and services her business provides. She needs a small map to add to the letters, but like many small startup businesses, she doesn't have a lot of money. She decides to design a basic map using a program she found on her Win 7 computer. She designs the map showing the railroad tracks near her house in the Paint program. She types her letters in WordPad and is then able to copy the map and paste the copy into her letters.

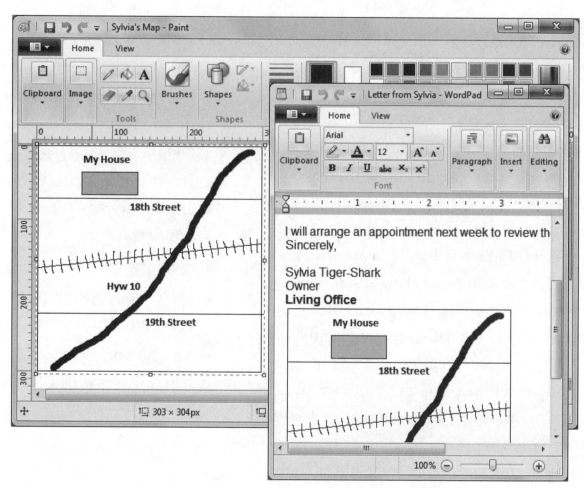

Paint, a picture-editing program, and WordPad, a word-processing program

Using Program Commands

Within programs, commands have traditionally been accessed from a series of drop-down menus on a menu bar or command buttons on a toolbar. In 2007, Microsoft introduced the "Windows Ribbon framework" in some of its programs as a new way to display commands. Win 7's versions of WordPad and Paint found in this book both use the newer ribbon feature.

Menu Commands

Drop-down menus are featured in most Windows-based programs. Menus are lists of commands traditionally organized in a series along a menu bar under the title bar. The first menu on most menu bars is the File menu, the second is the Edit menu, and the last is the Help menu. This is part of the traditional standardization found in Windows-based programs, such as the Notepad program used in this book.

Programs that use the newer ribbon system to display commands do not have a menu bar. There is a single menu button in the upper-left corner of the ribbon that replaces the File menu. The button is usually named for the program, for example Paint menu or WordPad menu. Rather than using a series of menus, other commands are accessed from a toolbar or the ribbon.

The following illustration shows some of the similarities and differences in the File menu in Notepad and the Paint menu in Paint.

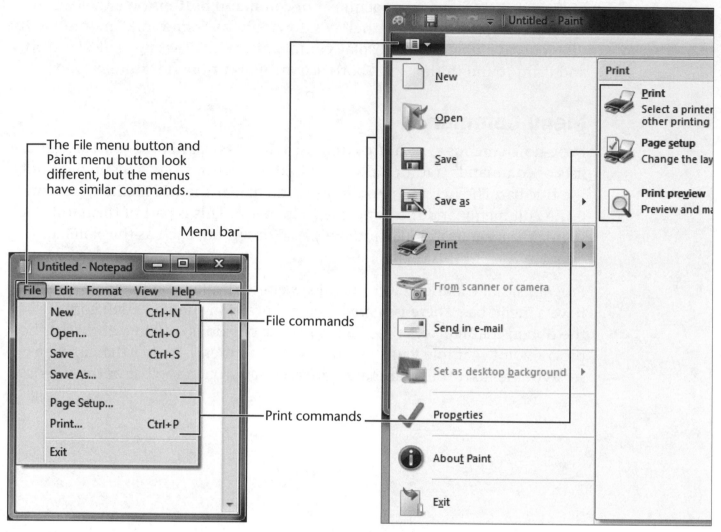

Notepad's File menu

Paint's Paint menu

Many of the commands in Notepad's File menu are standard to most programs, including Paint. On the other hand, Paint (a picture-editing program) has commands related to drawing or picture tasks, such as From Scanner or Camera or Set as Background, that do not appear in the File menu of Notepad (a word-processing program).

TIP! Menu commands do not always appear in the same order in different programs, and the text labels can vary.

HANDS-ON 3.1 **Compare Drop-Down Menus**

In this exercise, you will launch Notepad and Paint. You will compare common features in the File and Paint drop-down menus in these programs.

1. Open the Start ⊕ menu. Click Notepad if it is available in the left pane or click All Programs→Accessories→Notepad.

2. Repeat step 1, but this time to launch Paint.

3. Use the taskbar to make Notepad the active program window and then follow these steps to drop down the File menu in Notepad:

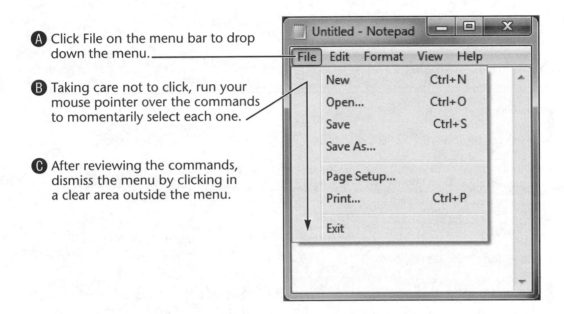

Ⓐ Click File on the menu bar to drop down the menu.

Ⓑ Taking care not to click, run your mouse pointer over the commands to momentarily select each one.

Ⓒ After reviewing the commands, dismiss the menu by clicking in a clear area outside the menu.

4. Make Paint the active program and then repeat step 3 with the Paint menu to compare its similarities and differences to Notepad's File menu.

Notice that the menus have common features, including New, Open, Save, Save As, Page Setup, Print, and Exit.

5. Compare the Notepad's traditional Edit menu with the Home tab on Paint's new ribbon where the commands Cut, Copy, and Paste have been relocated.

6. Close ▬ X ▬ Notepad, but leave Paint open.

Commands in Programs with Ribbons

Two of the programs used in this book, Paint and WordPad, have incorporated ribbons. In addition to commands in the program menu discussed above, these programs have commands on a Quick Access toolbar located on the title bar and commands on the ribbon arranged with a number of tabs.

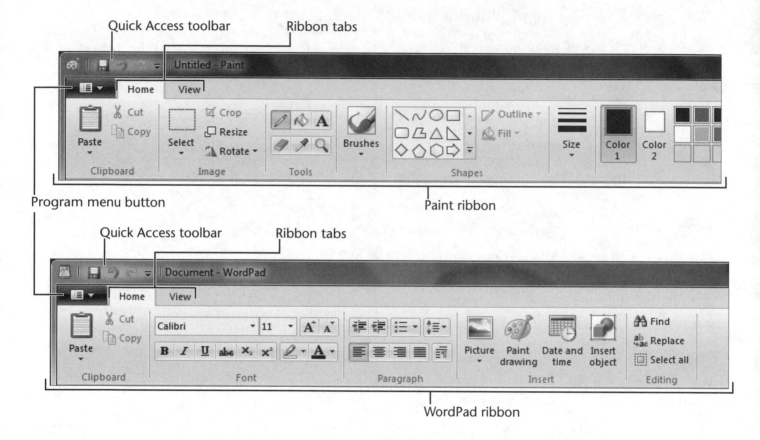

Both of these ribbons have features and some tools in common, but many tools are specific to each program's function—Paint to create and edit pictures and WordPad to create and edit text.

Quick Access Toolbar A toolbar is used to display series of commands as small buttons or drop-down lists. Commands on a toolbar or ribbon are often referred to as "tools." The Quick Access toolbar typically has three tools displayed: Save, Undo, and Redo. These commands will be discussed later.

Ribbon Tabs Paint and WordPad have only two ribbon tabs: Home and View. Other programs may have many more tabs.

A ribbon has many tools. Tabs on the ribbon are used to arrange tools by task. On each tab, related tools are assembled into command groups. Each command group has vertical separators and a label. Within each group tools can be displayed as buttons, drop-down lists, or galleries.

The icon for each tool attempts to indicate its purpose, but you can point over a tool to display its name and function on a ScreenTip.

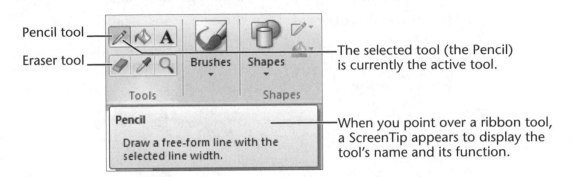

Pencil tool — The selected tool (the Pencil) is currently the active tool.

Eraser tool —

Pencil

Draw a free-form line with the selected line width.

When you point over a ribbon tool, a ScreenTip appears to display the tool's name and its function.

These three groups on a ribbon tab are divided with vertical separators and labeled: Tools, Brushes, and Shapes. A ScreenTip can identify a tool's name and function.

 TIP! If you are new to computers and still feel uncomfortable using a mouse, try drawing pictures and then carefully erasing lines in Paint. This is a fun and easy way to improve your mouse skills.

HANDS-ON 3.2 Draw in the Paint Program

In this exercise, you will draw a face and sign your name using the Pencil tool in Paint.

Before You Begin: Paint should be open from Hands-On 3.1.

1. Follow these steps to use a tool from the ribbon to draw a face and to sign your name:

Ⓐ Click the Home tab.

Ⓑ Point (don't click) over the Pencil tool in the Tools group to see its ScreenTip.

Ⓒ Click once to select the Pencil tool.

Ⓓ Point with the mouse pointer over the white canvas in the drawing area. The mouse pointer should look like a pencil.

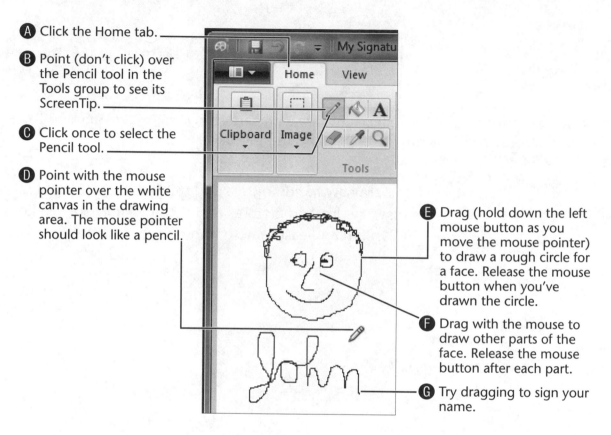

Ⓔ Drag (hold down the left mouse button as you move the mouse pointer) to draw a rough circle for a face. Release the mouse button when you've drawn the circle.

Ⓕ Drag with the mouse to draw other parts of the face. Release the mouse button after each part.

Ⓖ Try dragging to sign your name.

You will save your work in the next exercise.

⚠**NOTE!** If you don't like what you've drawn, choose the Eraser tool from the Tools group, drag to erase, and then choose the Pencil to try again.

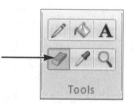

Saving Your Work

When you type a letter or create a drawing as you did in the previous exercise, you might want to save it so you can look at it later. The computer does not save your work unless you command it to do so. This section looks at two commands used to save your work: Save and Save As.

Where Your Work Is Located

In Lesson 1, Getting Your First Look, you learned that all of the things displayed on your screen are temporarily stored on the RAM chips of the computer. The work you have done so far in Paint is only temporarily stored in RAM. If the power goes out or the computer is shut down, the information in RAM will be erased, and your work will be lost.

You must save your work on a permanent storage device such as a hard drive or a USB flash drive to keep it from being erased. See the Behind the Screen: Drive Designations section on page 112 for descriptions of storage devices.

Win 7 needs to know two things the first time you save your work:

- What do you want to call it?

- Where do you want to store it?

Files and Folders

These two basic terms, files and folders, will be covered in more detail in the next lesson but need to be defined here.

- **File**—A file is collection of data stored with a name. Examples of files are a letter you've typed and saved, a drawing in Paint that you've saved, or a picture copied from the Internet.

- **Folder**—A folder is an electronic location in which you store related groups of files. For example, My Pictures and the Pictures library are folders already created for your username in Win 7 where you can store photos and other pictures.

Choosing a Storage Location

Today's computers provide a variety of storage choices, including internal and external hard drives, CDs, DVDs, and USB flash drives. When you are ready to save, you have an opportunity to choose which storage device you want to use. And remember, if you don't choose, the computer will choose for you (using what is called a *default* setting).

On the Internal Hard Drive   When saving your work (file) for the first time, most Win 7 programs will direct you to a predetermined location (folder) on the internal hard drive. On your home computer:

• WordPad directs you to a folder named Documents library.

• Paint directs you to a folder named Pictures library.

In most computer lab settings, students save their work on USB flash drives. This makes it easy to access files on your home computer as well.

Using the predetermined location is usually appropriate for new users until they learn more about Win 7's storage system. This will be covered in Lesson 4, Finding Files.

On a Portable USB Flash Drive   You can choose a different location from the one chosen by a program. Storing files on a USB flash drive (also called a thumb, pen, or keychain drive) has become a popular way to save files that need to be carried from one computer to another. A flash drive is a device with a USB plug attached to a storage card. The flash drive can be plugged into any USB port on a computer.

Connecting a flash drive to a computer

Creating a Filename

Data that is stored on a storage device is called a file. It might be a text document, a picture, a song, a movie, or any other kind of data. The first time you store data, it must be given a filename. The filename must follow Win 7's naming conventions (rules).

QUICK REFERENCE: Naming Files

Convention	Description
Filename length	Up to 255 characters
Allowed characters	All alphanumeric characters except those reserved
Reserved characters	| \ ? * < " : > /
Reserved words	aux, con, prn

 TIP! Choose a filename that will help you recognize the file's contents months from now. A filename like Letter to Ted Edwards is more useful than Ted Letter. If possible, keep the length less than 20 characters or so to make it easier to read in various windows and dialog boxes.

HANDS-ON 3.3 Save a New Document

In this exercise, you will save your Paint picture to your hard drive or USB flash drive for the first time. This will protect your work from a power failure.

Before You Begin: Paint should be open from Hands-On 3.2.

Name Your Picture

1. Make Paint the active program window.

2. Click the Paint menu 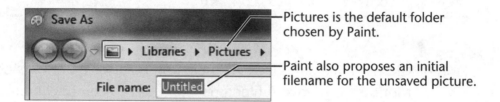 button and choose Save.

   Paint opens a Save As dialog box the first time a document is saved.

   Notice that Paint directs you to a Libraries folder (in this example Pictures) and has provided the temporary filename Untitled.

Pictures is the default folder chosen by Paint.

Paint also proposes an initial filename for the unsaved picture.

3. Follow the steps for your storage location to give your picture a filename:

The Pictures Folder on the Hard Drive

Ⓐ If the temporary filename is not already selected, double-click on the name to select it, and then type **My Signature**.

Ⓑ Click the Save button.

Paint saves your file to the hard drive. The new filename, My Signature, is displayed on the title bar.

Skip the rest of this exercise and continue reading the Save Versus Save As section on page 78.

Your USB Flash Drive

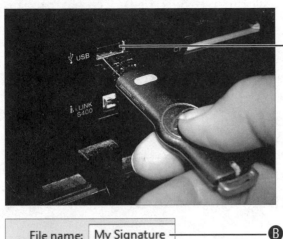

A Carefully place your USB flash drive into a USB port. This may be a port on the front or back of the computer, or there may be a cable you can plug the drive into. Your instructor or a classmate can help if necessary.

B If the temporary filename is not already selected, double-click on the name to select it and then type **My Signature**.

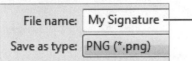

C Click the first drop-down list ▶ button on the Address bar. A list of storage locations drops down. Drop-down list buttons are often identified with a right-pointing arrow ▶ that, when clicked, becomes a down-pointing arrow ▼.

D Choose Computer from the list.

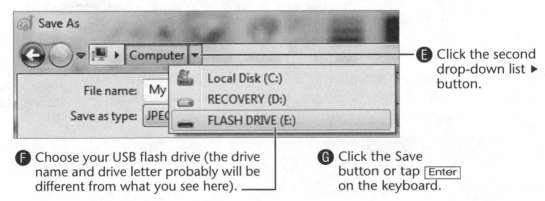

E Click the second drop-down list ▶ button.

F Choose your USB flash drive (the drive name and drive letter probably will be different from what you see here).

G Click the Save button or tap ⟨Enter⟩ on the keyboard.

A copy of My Signature is saved on your flash drive. The new filename, My Signature, is displayed on the title bar.

Save Versus Save As

The first time you save a document with the Save command, Win 7 opens a Save As dialog box to gather a filename and a storage location. After a file has been saved, choosing the Save command will save the changes without opening a dialog box because Win 7 already knows the filename and location.

The Save As command also is used to make a copy of a file in two ways:

- It lets you save an existing file with a different name (leaving the original file intact).

- It lets you save an existing file to another location (the filename can be the same or different).

 HANDS-ON 3.4 Use Save As to Create a Copy

In this exercise, you will create a copy of a file with a new filename using the Save As command.

Before You Begin: My Signature should be open in Paint from Hands-On 3.3.

1. Click the Paint menu button and choose Save As.

   > **!TIP!** In the rest of this book, program menu commands will be written like this:
   > Choose Paint menu →Save As.

   A Save As dialog box appears. The folder location shows where My Signature is saved, and the filename is selected and ready to be replaced.

2. Type the new filename **My Signature Copy**.

3. Click the Save button or tap ⎡Enter⎤ on the keyboard.
   A copy of My Signature is saved on the drive, and the new version is now displayed in the Paint window. The new filename, My Signature Copy, is displayed on the title bar.

   My Signature Copy – Paint

4. Close ⬛ X the Paint window. Choose Yes or Save if you are prompted to save any changes.

Using the Work Area

Up to this point, you have concentrated on features on the perimeter of program windows, such as borders, menus, and control buttons. These are the tools that help when you are working in a program. Now you will look more closely at the work area, the place where you use the tools and do the work.

Mouse Pointers

In the previous exercise, you saw that the mouse pointer looked like a pencil when the Pencil tool was active. This Win 7 feature changes the appearance of the mouse pointer when the function of the mouse pointer has changed.

QUICK REFERENCE: Using Win 7 Mouse Pointers

Mouse Pointer	Function
↖	Normal selection pointer
I	Text selection pointer
+	Precision selection pointer
○	System busy pointer
✥	Move pointer
↕	Vertical resize pointer

Tool Galleries

Many tool groups in Paint include galleries. A gallery is a collection of tools or options. Tools in a gallery may be shown in full view or partial view or may be hidden from view as a button on the ribbon. If part of the gallery is in view, a scroll bar is provided to view other tools. If a gallery has been hidden, its gallery button will display a downward-pointing arrow. The button must be selected for its drop-down gallery to be displayed.

 TIP! Users new to a program with a ribbon will find it easier to use the ribbon if the window is maximized. Some tool groups and galleries compress to become only buttons as a window is made smaller.

Paint will remember the most recently selected choice the next time you use that tool. Also, be aware that options such as line thickness in the Size gallery can change when different tools are selected.

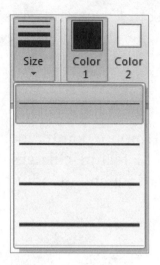

The line thickness options in the Size gallery available when Pencil is the active tool.

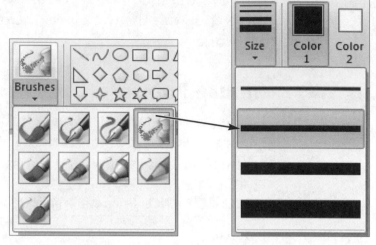

Airbrush is the selected tool in this drop-down Brushes gallery.

Size options are different when Airbrush has been made the active tool.

 HANDS-ON 3.5   Change Mouse Pointers in Paint

In this exercise, you will select different tools from the Paint program ribbon and observe appearance changes to the mouse pointer as you create a drawing.

1. Open Paint again with Start ⊕ →All Programs→Accessories→Paint.

2. Maximize ▣ the window and then click the Home tab.

3. Click the buttons in the Tools group one at a time and move your mouse over the white canvas to see the mouse pointer.

   Notice the changing appearance of the mouse pointer.

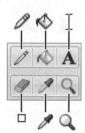

4. Follow these steps to step up options for the Rectangle tool:

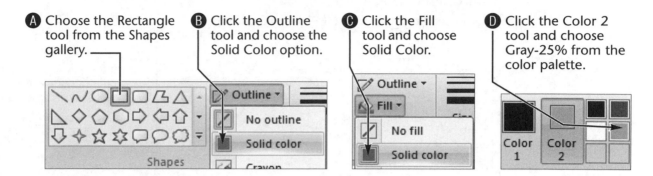

(A) Choose the Rectangle tool from the Shapes gallery.

(B) Click the Outline tool and choose the Solid Color option.

(C) Click the Fill tool and choose Solid Color.

(D) Click the Color 2 tool and choose Gray-25% from the color palette.

5. Point near the top of the drawing area and then drag down and to the right to make a box, as shown below.

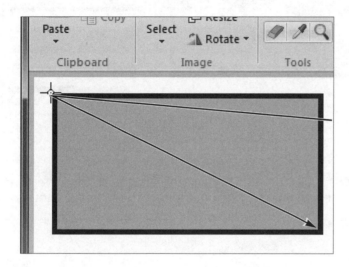

The line color is determined by the Color 1 choice; the fill color is determined by the Color 2 choice.

6. Follow these steps to set up and use the Eraser tool:

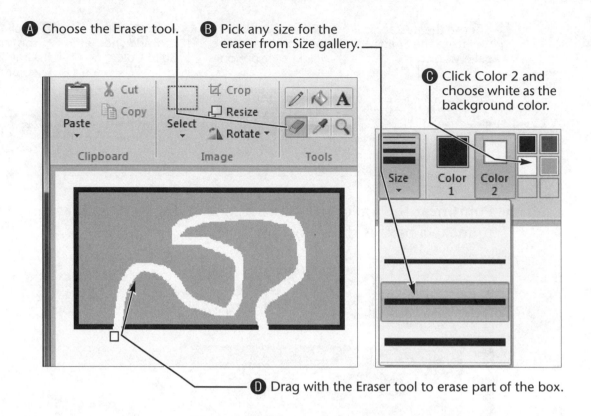

Ⓐ Choose the Eraser tool. Ⓑ Pick any size for the eraser from Size gallery.

Ⓒ Click Color 2 and choose white as the background color.

Ⓓ Drag with the Eraser tool to erase part of the box.

Notice that the mouse pointer changes to reflect the size and color of the Eraser. The Eraser tool does not actually erase; rather, it paints the Color 2 choice.

Scroll Bars

When part of your picture or content is too large be seen in the program window, Win 7 will display scroll bars. A vertical scroll bar will let you move up or down, and a horizontal scroll bar will let you move side to side.

Each scroll bar has three parts:

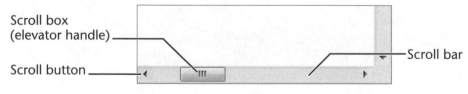

Scroll box (elevator handle)

Scroll button

Scroll bar

Horizontal and vertical scroll bars

HANDS-ON 3.6 Use Scroll Bars

In this exercise, you will resize the Paint window and use the vertical and horizontal scroll bars.

1. Maximize ▣ the Paint window.

   Are scroll bars displayed? Probably not, unless you have a very small computer screen (which isn't likely on a new Win 7 computer).

2. Restore down ▣ the Paint window and then drag the bottom-right corner sizing handle to make the window small enough to see both scroll bars.

3. Follow these steps to practice scrolling up and down:

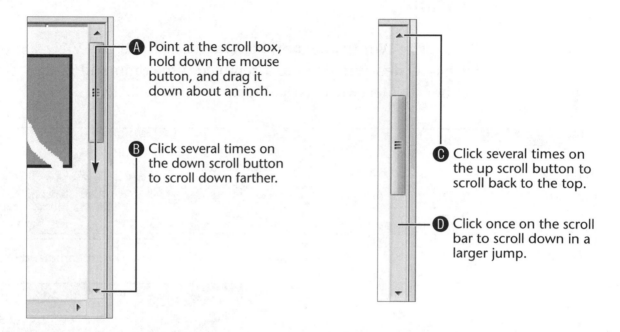

Ⓐ Point at the scroll box, hold down the mouse button, and drag it down about an inch.

Ⓑ Click several times on the down scroll button to scroll down farther.

Ⓒ Click several times on the up scroll button to scroll back to the top.

Ⓓ Click once on the scroll bar to scroll down in a larger jump.

4. Try using parts of the horizontal scroll bar to scroll from side to side.

5. Minimize ▭ the Paint program window.

Typing with WordPad

WordPad is a basic word processing program included with Win 7 that is used to type letters and other simple documents. Although it is a basic program, it makes an excellent learning program because it has many features common to other applications.

WordPad Ribbon

Like the Paint program, the Win 7 version of WordPad now uses a ribbon instead of the traditional system of a menu bar and toolbars. Many of the features used in WordPad ribbon are like those found in Microsoft Word 2007 and 2010.

Tabs   The WordPad ribbon has two tabs: Home and View. On each tab, tools with a related function are assembled into command groups, which are further divided with vertical separators and labeled.

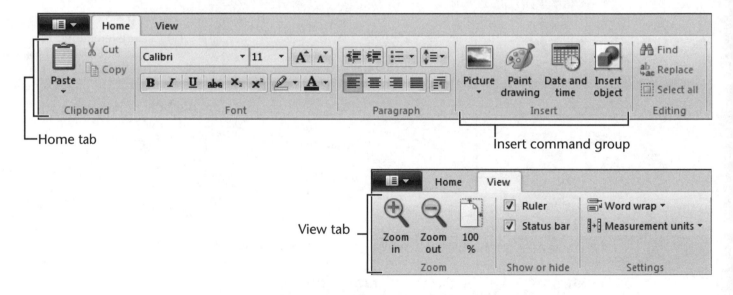

Related tools on each tab are assembled into command groups, divided with separators, and labeled.

Drop-Down Lists   WordPad has several drop-down lists on the Home tab. Three frequently used drop-down lists are located in the Font group: Font family, Font size, and Font color. The purpose of a drop-down list is to offer other choices. A button with a down-pointing arrow is provided to view the choices. Some drop-down lists (such as Font family) are quite long and include a scroll bar.

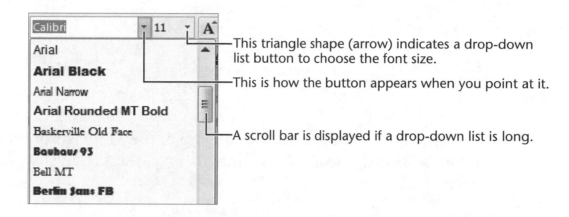

This triangle shape (arrow) indicates a drop-down list button to choose the font size.

This is how the button appears when you point at it.

A scroll bar is displayed if a drop-down list is long.

ScreenTips   Just as you saw with Paint, WordPad's ScreenTips help you determine the function of tools or drop-down lists on the ribbon. When you rest your mouse pointer over a tool or drop-down list, a ScreenTip will appear with its name and a brief description.

A ScreenTip with a name and brief description appears when the mouse pointer rests over a button.

TIP!   When you discover a useful feature such as ScreenTips in one program, check to see if the same feature is used in other programs.

The Cursor and the Mouse Pointer

New users can be confused in word-processing programs such as WordPad by what appear to be two cursors: One is the blinking *cursor* in the text and the other is the *mouse pointer* (which can be most anywhere you point). The blinking cursor is often also called the *insertion point*. When you type, the text goes in front of the blinking cursor.

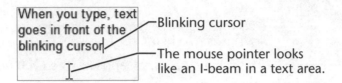

When you type, text goes in front of the blinking cursor ——Blinking cursor

——The mouse pointer looks like an I-beam in a text area.

The blinking cursor is located at the top of the white writing area when WordPad is first opened. This white writing area is equivalent to a sheet of paper.

 TIP! Most of the word-processing skills learned in this lesson can be used to type email and in most other word-processing programs.

Special Keys on the Keyboard

Computer keyboards are more complex than those of typewriters. Some keys on the keyboard of a computer have special functions and are not found on any typewriter.

Backspace and Delete Keys   On a typewriter, backspace is used to move backward through the text. The Backspace key on a computer keyboard erases text to the left of the cursor. The Delete key erases text to the right of the cursor.

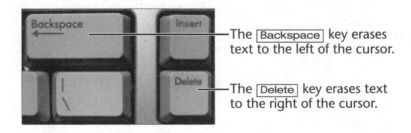

The Backspace key erases text to the left of the cursor.

The Delete key erases text to the right of the cursor.

Tab Key The [Tab] key is similar to the tab key on a typewriter. It moves the cursor right to the next half-inch mark on the ruler. This is a useful key for creating accurately aligned columns.

Enter Key The [Enter] key has two functions: It ends a paragraph and moves any text below or to the right of the cursor down one line.

HANDS-ON 3.7 **Practice Basic Typing in WordPad**

In this exercise, you will do basic typing using the [Tab], [Spacebar], and [Enter] keys; correct mistakes using the [Backspace] and [Delete] keys; and move around using the [Home], [End], and arrow keys.

1. If necessary, click the WordPad window to make it active.

2. Type the following:

To: [Tab] **Ted** [Spacebar] **Edwards** [Enter]
From: [Tab] **Margo** [Spacebar] **Collie** [Enter]
[Enter]
Dear [Spacebar] **Ted,**

Notice that using the [Tab] key aligns the both first names to the half-inch mark on the ruler. The [Spacebar] puts a space between words. When [Enter] is typed once, it ends a paragraph and moves the cursor down to a new line. When the [Enter] key is typed twice in succession, the second [Enter] creates a blank line and moves the cursor down to a second new line.

3. Tap [Enter] twice.
This creates two new lines.

4. Type the following:

If I type a sentence that is too long to fit on one line, I do not have to tap the Enter key when I get near the margin because the words will automatically wrap to a new line. [Enter]
[Enter]
Typing is fun.

Most email and word-processing programs will automatically wrap text.
It is necessary to tap [Enter] only when you want to end a paragraph and force text to start on a new line.

Editing Text

One advantage of computerized word processing over mechanical typing on a typewriter is the ability to extensively edit and format the text before it is printed. When you are typing text, concentrate on getting your ideas typed first and worry about spelling, grammar, and layout later.

 TIP! When typing a letter or a story, you do not have to stop and make corrections as you type. You can always make corrections later. If you stop to correct errors, you break your train of thought and may forget some important ideas.

Selecting Text

Text must be *selected* before it can be edited (changed). Selecting text lets the computer know which part of the text to change. When text is selected, it will typically become highlighted as though it were marked with a black or blue highlighter pen.

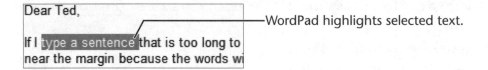
WordPad highlights selected text.

There may be more than one way to select the same text. You will become more productive if you become familiar with different selection methods.

QUICK REFERENCE: Selecting Text

Selection Procedure	Result
Drag with mouse	Selects a letter, a word, a sentence, or a paragraph
Double-click	Selects a word
Triple-click	Selects an entire paragraph
Home tab→Select All	Selects an entire document

HANDS-ON 3.8 **Select Text in WordPad**

In this exercise, you will select text different ways: dragging with the mouse, clicking with the mouse, and using ribbon commands.

Before You Begin: WordPad should still be open from Hands-On 3.7.

1. Follow these steps for selecting text:

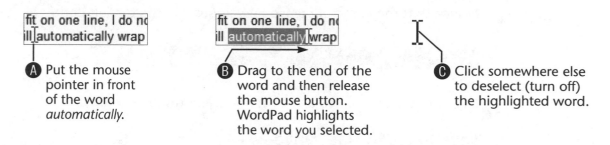

A Put the mouse pointer in front of the word *automatically*.

B Drag to the end of the word and then release the mouse button. WordPad highlights the word you selected.

C Click somewhere else to deselect (turn off) the highlighted word.

2. Point over the word *automatically* and double-click.

   WordPad selects the entire word and the space after the word. This is a bit easier than dragging to select the single word.

3. Click away from the word to deselect it.

4. Drag over the entire first paragraph to select the whole paragraph and then click away to deselect it.

5. Point over the first paragraph and triple-click to select the whole paragraph; click away to deselect it.

   When you triple-click, you do not have to click rapidly. Just click three times smoothly without moving the mouse. WordPad selects the entire paragraph.

6. To select all of the text in the document, choose Home tab→Editing→Select All and then click away to deselect.

Save Your Work

When you finish a significant piece of work on a document, it's always a good idea to save it.

7. Choose WordPad menu→Save to save the document.

   WordPad displays the Save As dialog box. The temporary name, Document, is selected and ready to be replaced.

8. Type the new filename **Memo to Ted Edwards**.

9. Follow the appropriate steps to store the file on the hard drive or the USB flash drive:

Save to the Hard Drive

- Click the Save button or tap ⎡Enter⎤ on the keyboard.

WordPad saves your letter to the Documents folder on the hard drive. (This is a default setting, meaning that it is the setting WordPad will use unless you indicate otherwise.) Notice that the name of the file now appears in the top-left corner of the title bar.

Skip the rest of this step and continue reading the next topic.

Save to a USB Flash Drive

Ⓐ Click the drop-down list ▸ button and choose Computer.

Ⓑ Click the second drop-down list ▸ button and choose your USB flash drive.

Ⓒ Click the Save button or tap ⎡Enter⎤ on the keyboard.

WordPad saves your letter to the USB flash drive. You may see a small light flash on the drive, indicating that Win 7 is working on a file there. Notice that the name of the file now appears in the top-left corner of the title bar.

Formatting Text

Another task you can perform when editing your text is formatting. Formatting text in WordPad includes choosing a text style (Font family), text size (Font size, Grow font, or Shrink font), text style (**Bold**, *Italic*, <u>Underline</u>), and text color (Text color). These button or drop-down list choices can be found on the Home tab in the Font group.

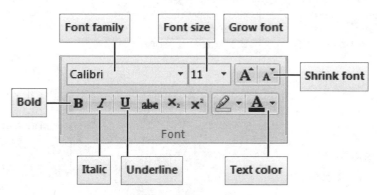

The Font group on the Home tab in WordPad

!NOTE! In most word processing programs, you will need to select the text you want to format *before* you choose formatting changes.

Live Preview   Many options on the ribbon have a new feature called Live Preview. Text must first be selected for Live Preview to work. As you point the mouse over each option, the selected text will instantly change to display that option's appearance.

HANDS-ON 3.9 Format Text in WordPad

In this exercise, you will change formatting using various buttons and drop-down lists.

Before You Begin: WordPad should still be open from Hands-On 3.8.

1. Follow these steps to make formatting changes to the text you have typed:

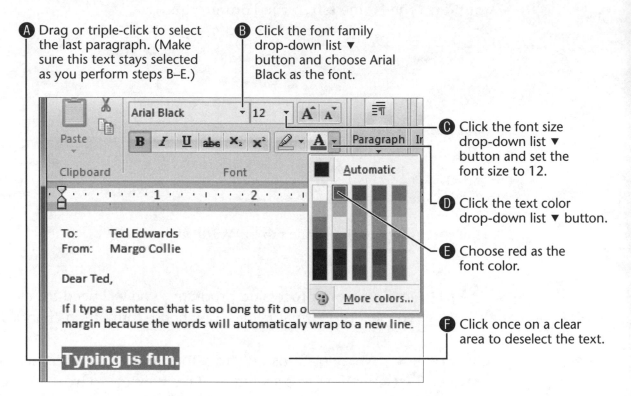

A Drag or triple-click to select the last paragraph. (Make sure this text stays selected as you perform steps B–E.)

B Click the font family drop-down list ▼ button and choose Arial Black as the font.

C Click the font size drop-down list ▼ button and set the font size to 12.

D Click the text color drop-down list ▼ button.

E Choose red as the font color.

F Click once on a clear area to deselect the text.

As you can see, as long as the text remains selected, you can repeatedly apply formatting commands to it. Also, you can see that Live Preview changes the selected text's format as you move your mouse across different options on the drop-down lists.

2. Follow these steps to format a single word:

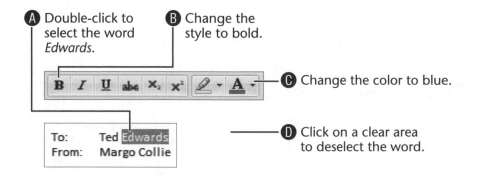

A Double-click to select the word *Edwards*.

B Change the style to bold.

C Change the color to blue.

D Click on a clear area to deselect the word.

It's easy to select and format single words.

Printing a Document

You may want to print a drawing or a letter you have created. Win 7 provides three commands to help you print:

- **Print Preview**—Preview the document on the monitor and make changes before you print
- **Quick Print**—Send the document directly to the printer without any changes
- **Print**—Select the printer, pages to print, number of copies, and other options before printing

Print commands can be accessed on the File menu and sometimes with buttons on a toolbar or on the Program menu in programs with a ribbon.

 HANDS-ON 3.10 **Print a Document**

In this exercise, you will preview the Memo to Ted Edward and then print it.

Before You Begin: WordPad should still be open from Hands-On 3.9.

1. Choose WordPad menu 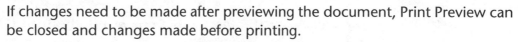 →Print→Print Preview.

   The document is displayed as it will appear on the paper when printed.

2. Position the mouse over the memo text, click once, and then click again.

   Each time you click the memo with the mouse, Win 7 zooms in to make reading easier or zooms out to see the layout of the document on the page.

3. Click the Close Print Preview command to close the Print Preview screen.

   If changes need to be made after previewing the document, Print Preview can be closed and changes made before printing.

4. Choose WordPad menu 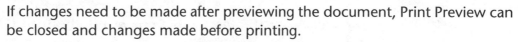 →Print→Print.

5. Follow these steps to print the document:

Ⓐ Choose All in the Page Range area, if necessary. Notice other options available.

Ⓑ Choose 1 in the Number of Copies box. Notice the increment and decrement buttons on the right to increase or decrease the number.

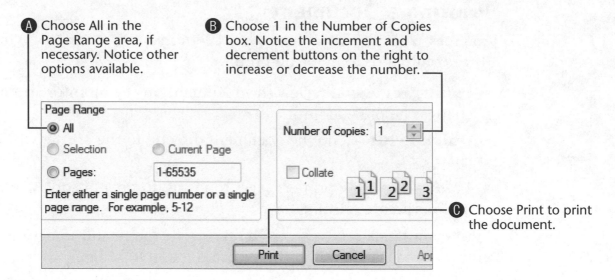

Ⓒ Choose Print to print the document.

6. Leave WordPad open.

Using Cut, Copy, and Paste

Most Win 7 programs support the Cut, Copy, and Paste commands. The Cut, Copy, and Paste commands in WordPad are found in the Clipboard group on the Home tab.

- **Cut** deletes a selected object from its present location and places a copy of the object in a special folder called Clipboard.

- **Copy** places a copy of a selected object in Clipboard without deleting it from its present location.

- **Paste** inserts a copy of the last object cut or copied into the present location of the cursor.

- **Cut and Paste** used together let you move text and other objects from one place in a program to another place within the same program (or to another program).

- **Copy and Paste** used together let you copy text or another object from one place in a program to another place within the same program (or to another program).

> **TIP!** You can move text that has been selected by dragging and dropping the selected text at a new location. You can copy text that has been selected by dragging and dropping the selected text at a new location while holding down the ⌐Ctrl¬ key.

QUICK REFERENCE: Using Cut or Copy and Paste Commands

Task	Procedure
Use Cut or Copy and Paste	• Select the text or object you want to move or copy. • Choose Home tab→Cut or Home tab→Copy to place a copy in Clipboard. • Place the cursor where you want to paste the text or object from Clipboard. • Choose Home tab→Paste. • You can paste the text or object again by repeating the preceding two steps.

 HANDS-ON 3.11 **Practice Using Cut, Copy, and Paste**

In this exercise, you will cut and paste text to move it within a WordPad document and then create a signature in Paint and place a copy into WordPad using Copy and Paste.

Before You Begin: WordPad should still be open from Hands-On 3.10.

Use Cut and Paste

1. Follow these steps to move a paragraph using Cut and Paste:

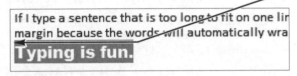

Ⓐ Drag or triple-click to select the last paragraph.

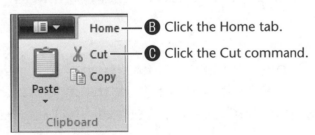

Ⓑ Click the Home tab.

Ⓒ Click the Cut command.

WordPad cuts the text to Clipboard, and the text disappears from the document. Now that the text is in Clipboard, you can paste it to a new location.

2. Click once at the end of the last sentence to place the blinking cursor, as shown here.

If I type a sentence that is too long to fit on one line, I do not have to tap the Enter key when I get near the margin because the words will automatically wrap to a new line.

Placing the cursor in the document tells WordPad where you want your next command (Paste) to be performed.

3. Choose Home tab→Paste from the ribbon.

WordPad pastes the text from Clipboard back into the document.

4. Tap the [Enter] key twice and then choose Home tab→Paste from the ribbon again.

WordPad pastes the text again. Whatever you cut or copy to Clipboard remains there until you cut or copy something else, so you can paste the same item repeatedly if you wish.

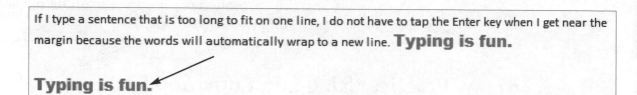

5. Choose Undo ↺ from the Quick Access toolbar.

WordPad undoes your most recent command, in this case Paste.

6. Position the I-beam behind the last sentence and drag to select the words *Typing is fun.*

7. Place your mouse over the selected text, hold down the left mouse button, drag the mouse pointer down to the beginning of the next line, and release.

The text has been moved.

8. Choose Undo ↺ from the Quick Access toolbar to undo the move.

Use Copy and Paste

9. Place your mouse over the selected text and repeat step 7, but this time also hold down the [Ctrl] key until after you release the mouse button.

This time the text has been copied because the [Ctrl] key was being held down.

10. Choose Undo ↺ from the Quick Access toolbar to undo the copy.

11. Click the Paint program button on the Win 7 taskbar to make it the active program.

12. Choose Paint menu ▦▾ →New.

Paint asks if you wish to save the changes.

13. Choose Don't Save.

Paint displays a new, clear drawing canvas for your next drawing.

14. Follow these step to create a signature in Paint:

> ⚠️ **NOTE!** Don't forget that you can use Undo 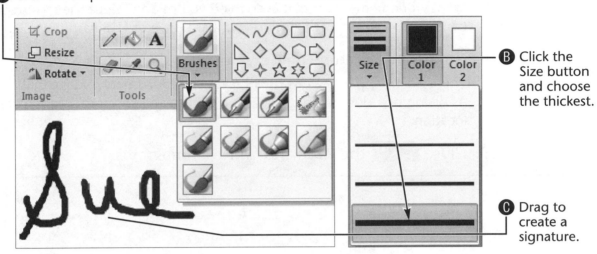 from the Quick Access toolbar to undo a Paint command. If you don't like a line just drawn, undo it and try again.

Ⓐ Click the drop-down arrow on the Brushes button and choose Brush.

Ⓑ Click the Size button and choose the thickest.

Ⓒ Drag to create a signature.

Now that you've created your signature, you can copy it to Clipboard for pasting into WordPad.

15. Follow these steps to copy your signature to Clipboard:

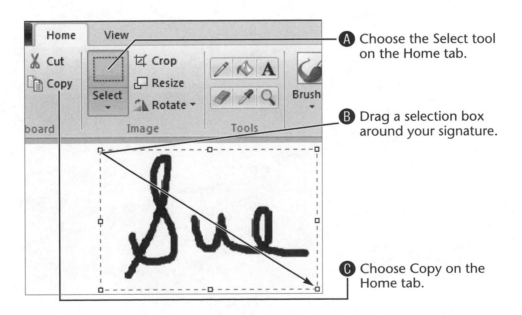

Ⓐ Choose the Select tool on the Home tab.

Ⓑ Drag a selection box around your signature.

Ⓒ Choose Copy on the Home tab.

16. Use the WordPad button on the taskbar to make WordPad active.

17. Place the cursor on the last blank line in WordPad and choose Paste on the Home tab.

Your signature appears at the bottom of the text. It's usually this easy to copy and paste from one program into a different program.

Save Your Work

Now that you have finished editing this document, you want to be sure to save your latest work. Remember that everything you've done since the most recent Save command is still in RAM, not on your hard drive or USB flash drive.

18. Choose WordPad menu [icon] →Save.

There is a brief pause as WordPad saves your document. Notice that this time the Save As dialog box does not appear. This is because you've already given the file a name and location.

19. Close [X] the Paint and WordPad programs.

Concepts Review

True/False Questions

1. The Backspace key moves the cursor to the left without erasing text.   **true**   **false**   _____

2. Cut and Paste commands let you move selections from one place to another.   **true**   **false**   _____

3. A flash drive can be plugged into any USB port.   **true**   **false**   _____

4. When typing text, new text goes in front of the I-beam mouse pointer and not in front of the blinking cursor.   **true**   **false**   _____

5. Saving a file takes it from RAM and places a copy onto a drive.   **true**   **false**   _____

6. "My current letter-22" is a valid filename.   **true**   **false**   _____

Multiple Choice Questions

1. Which command lets you reverse your most recent task?
   Page number: _____
   a. Undo
   b. Cut
   c. Paste
   d. Save

2. The feature on the side and bottom of a program window that lets you navigate through the document is called a(n) _____.
   Page number: _____
   a. elevator bar
   b. scroll bar
   c. zoom bar
   d. view bar

3. Before you save your work in a program for the first time, where is it located?
   Page number: _____
   a. On the hard drive
   b. On the USB flash drive
   c. In RAM
   d. In the monitor

4. You use the Save As command to _____.
   Page number: _____
   a. save a copy of a file to different location
   b. save a copy of a file with a different name
   c. save an unsaved file with a name and to a location of your choice
   d. All of the above

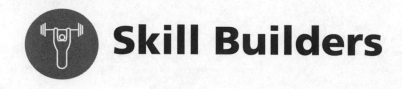

Skill Builders

SKILL BUILDER 3.1 **Create and Save a Letter from Start to Finish**

In this exercise, you will create, edit, and format a letter for Sylvia to use in her goldfish aquarium business and save it to your hard drive or flash drive (thumb drive).

1. Open WordPad using Start→All Programs→Accessories→WordPad.

2. Maximize ▣ the WordPad window if necessary.

3. Type the following letter. You can use the Backspace and Delete keys to correct errors as you type or wait until you are finished to select mistyped words and replace them.

> **Dear Business Owner,** [Enter]
> [Enter]
> **Thank you for your interest in having an aquarium placed in your main lobby. I have enclosed a price list for the aquariums I have available. All prices include initial setup of the aquarium, the first group of goldfish, and appropriate aquatic plants.** [Enter]
> [Enter]
> **Unless you have qualified staff to maintain the aquarium, I recommend our affordable monthly service. Our service is guaranteed.** [Enter]
> [Enter]
> **I will arrange an appointment next week to review the details.** [Enter]
> **Sincerely,** [Enter]
> [Enter]
> **Sylvia Tiger-Shark** [Enter]
> **Owner** [Enter]
> **Living Office** [Enter]

Edit the Letter

4. If you have not done so already, select any errors and replace them with correct text.

5. Choose Home tab→Select All from the ribbon to select all text in the document.

   WordPad highlights all the text you've typed, ready for your next command.

6. Use the Font Size to change the font size to 12 pt.

7. Click once somewhere in the document to deselect the text.

8. Select the words *Living Office* on the last line and make them bold.

Save the Letter

9. Choose Save 🖫 from the Quick Access toolbar to save the document.

   WordPad displays the Save As dialog box. The temporary name, Document, is selected and ready to be replaced.

10. Type a new filename: `Letter from Sylvia`.

11. Follow the appropriate steps to store the file on the hard drive or the USB flash drive:

Save to the Hard Drive

   • Click the Save 🖫 button or tap ⌨Enter on the keyboard.

   WordPad saves your letter to the Documents folder on the hard drive. (This is a default setting, meaning that it is the setting WordPad will use unless you indicate otherwise.)

   Skip the rest of this step and continue with the next exercise.

Save to a USB Flash Drive

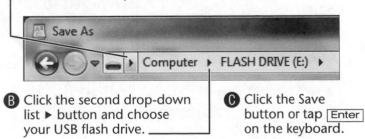

Ⓐ Click the drop-down list ▶ button and choose Computer.

Ⓑ Click the second drop-down list ▶ button and choose your USB flash drive.

Ⓒ Click the Save button or tap ⌨Enter on the keyboard.

   Leave WordPad open to use in the next exercise.

Create a Map for Your Letter

In this exercise, you will create a map in Paint and paste it into the letter created in Hands-On 3.1.

1. Open Paint (Start→All Programs→Accessories→Paint).

2. Maximize ▣ the Paint window.

3. Choose View tab→Rulers if rulers are not displayed.

Rulers in Paint are marked in pixels (px) because digital pictures are made up of pixels.

Make a Map

4. Choose Home tab and use the following steps to create a small map (you can be creative):

> ⚠️ **TIP!** As you try these tools, *you will make mistakes*. Remember to immediately use Undo on the Quick Access toolbar to undo the mistake. You may want to use [Ctrl] + [Z] from the keyboard to undo (hold down [Ctrl] and tap [Z]). Undo

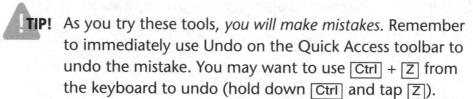

Ⓐ Choose Shapes→Rectangle. Set options: Outline→Solid, Fill→No Fill, Size→Thinnest.

Ⓒ Choose Brushes→Brush. Set option: Size→Thickest.

Ⓔ Choose Shapes→Line. Set option: Size→Thinnest.

Ⓖ Choose Tools→Pencil. Set option: Size→Thinnest.

Ⓘ Choose Shapes→Rectangle. Set options: Outline→Solid, Fill→Solid, Color 2→ Gray 25%.

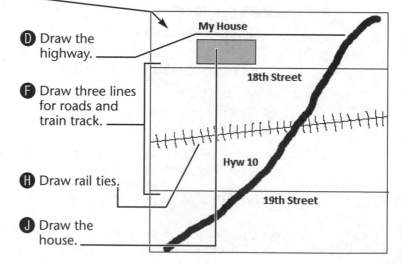

Ⓑ Drag a small map area about 300px by 300px from the upper-left corner of the canvas.

Ⓓ Draw the highway.

Ⓕ Draw three lines for roads and train track.

Ⓗ Draw rail ties.

Ⓙ Draw the house.

My House

18th Street

Hyw 10

19th Street

5. Follow these steps to add text to the map:

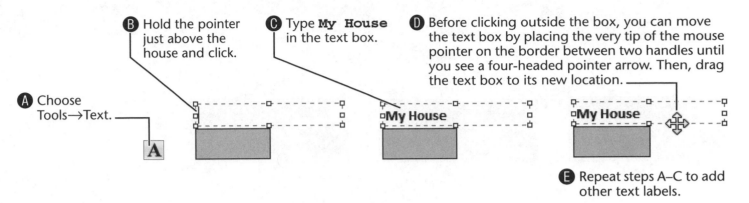

B Hold the pointer just above the house and click.

C Type **My House** in the text box.

D Before clicking outside the box, you can move the text box by placing the very tip of the mouse pointer on the border between two handles until you see a four-headed pointer arrow. Then, drag the text box to its new location.

A Choose Tools→Text.

□My House

□My House

E Repeat steps A–C to add other text labels.

6. Choose Paint menu [icon] →Save, name the file **Map**, and save to your flash drive.

Copy and Paste the Map

7. Choose Image→Select and drag a selection box around the map.

8. Choose Clipboard→Copy.

9. Make WordPad the active window and place the cursor below *Living Office*.

10. Choose Home tab→Clipboard→Paste.

The map appears below *Living Office*.

Save Your Work

Now that you've finished the letter and picture, it's time to finish your multitasking session by saving your work and closing the program windows.

11. Choose WordPad menu [icon] →Save.

WordPad saves the latest version of the document with the picture in it.

12. Close [X] the WordPad program window. Choose Save if you are prompted to save any changes.

13. Close [X] the Paint window. Choose Save if you are prompted to save any changes.

File Management

In this unit, you will deal with file management. You will begin by learning about how files, folders, and drives are organized on the computer. You will also work with Win 7's search tools so you know how to locate files that have been misplaced. You will also organize your own files in folders and subfolders and learn how to move and delete files and folders. Finally, you will make copies of your files and save them to portable storage devices.

Finding Files

Finding your files when you need them is obviously important. You will know where to find a file you create if you take note of the folder location the first time a file is saved. You also will need to understand how files, folders, and drives are organized on your computer so you can navigate through the drive and folder system. Finally, you need to become familiar with the search tools in Win 7 that can help you find files that have been misplaced.

LESSON OBJECTIVES

After studying this lesson, you will be able to:

- Describe and use various storage devices

- Use Explorer to locate files and folders

- Plug in and properly unplug a USB flash drive

- Identify different types of folders used by Win 7

- Find files and folders with Windows Search

*Additional learning resources are available at **labpub.com/learn/silver/wtw7/***

Case Study: Checking Up on the Hard Drive

Jamal has had his computer for a while, and he is becoming concerned about two potential problems:

- Since he bought a digital camera, he thinks the pictures he has been saving on his computer may fill the hard drive to its maximum capacity.

- He also worries that all of his files would be lost if he had a fire in his house or if the hard drive in his computer failed.

A friend suggested that Jamal could save backup copies of the files on one or more external hard drives. Because an external hard drive is portable, he could keep it in his office at work. The external hard drive at work would keep the backup copies of his files safe from disasters at home.

Jamal first wanted to determine the capacity of his hard drive and how much of it was being used. His friend showed him how to determine the capacity of the hard drive by looking at its Properties box. It looked like this:

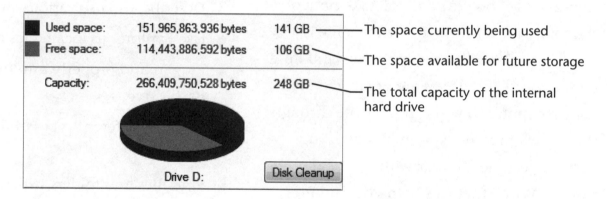

Jamal could see that the drive was more than half full. He decided to buy an external hard drive with a capacity of at least 500 GB and start backing up his files on the new drive on a regular basis.

Learning About Storage Media

On most computers, you have many options for saving files you have created. Some of these storage devices are internal (inside the computer) and can't be moved. Others are portable and can be moved from computer to computer.

Types of Storage Devices

All of these devices can be used to store the various types of files you create, including documents, pictures, music, and videos.

Internal Hard Drive   This is the *permanent* storage inside the computer. Most of your files and all of the software that runs on your computer reside on this internal drive.

CD/DVD Drives   You can save files and folders on CDs or DVDs just like the ones your music and movies are delivered on. CDs and DVDs are used to store files because of their large storage capacity and their portability.

External Hard Drives You can purchase hard drives that plug into your computer through a USB port (drives are discussed in the Behind the Screen: Drive Designations section on page 112). These external drives work just like internal hard drives with the added advantage of being portable, enabling you to access your files on multiple computers.

Photo courtesy of Western Digital Corporation

USB Flash Drives USB flash drives are sometimes referred to as keychain drives or thumb drives. These small, key-sized drives allow you to easily carry files between computers at home, at work, or anywhere.

Network Drives Sometimes your computer will be connected to hard drives on other computers via a network. Although network drives may be located in another room or another building, these remote drives can be used just like an internal drive or a portable storage device plugged into a USB port.

Viewing Storage Drives in Win 7

In an office, you might store your files in a filing cabinet. The filing cabinet could have one drawer or many drawers. Storage on your computer is similar. Each storage device is like a drawer in a filing cabinet. Most Win 7 computers will have two or more drives included: an internal hard drive and a CD/DVD burner. If you attach a USB flash drive to your computer, it is like having another drawer in which you can store data. Computers attached to a network may have access to several more drives.

Drive Letters   Win 7 provides an orderly process to deal with multiple drives. Each drive is assigned a *drive letter* to help identify it. Obviously, you need to be able to view the drives and their drive letters, as well as the data stored on the drives, for them to be useful. Windows Explorer is the Win 7 feature that lets you view the drives and their data. (Explorer is covered in more detail later in this lesson.)

Viewing the Drives   The Computer window lets you view the drives and then open the drives to see the data stored on them. In the figure below, Explorer has grouped the hard disk drives and the devices with removable storage. It also has displayed the drive names, drive letters, and additional information about drive capacity.

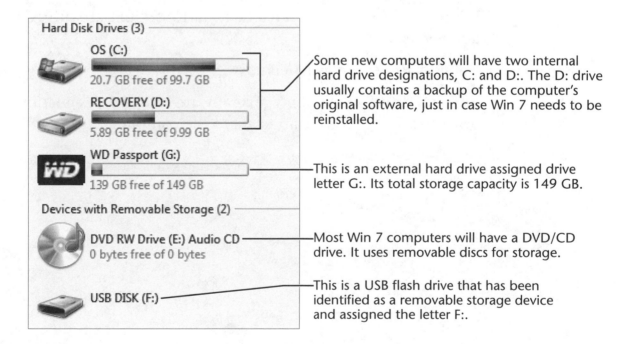

Hard Disk Drives (3)

OS (C:)
20.7 GB free of 99.7 GB

RECOVERY (D:)
5.89 GB free of 9.99 GB

WD Passport (G:)
139 GB free of 149 GB

Devices with Removable Storage (2)

DVD RW Drive (E:) Audio CD
0 bytes free of 0 bytes

USB DISK (F:)

Some new computers will have two internal hard drive designations, C: and D:. The D: drive usually contains a backup of the computer's original software, just in case Win 7 needs to be reinstalled.

This is an external hard drive assigned drive letter G:. Its total storage capacity is 149 GB.

Most Win 7 computers will have a DVD/CD drive. It uses removable discs for storage.

This is a USB flash drive that has been identified as a removable storage device and assigned the letter F:.

Drive Designations

History   Storage devices or drives in the computer are designated with letters of the alphabet followed by a colon (:). The alphabet letter and colon combination has been around since the early beginnings of computers, when there were no graphic images to represent drives.

What Determines Drive Order?   There are logical reasons why drives are assigned certain letters—at least for the first few drives in your computer.

Drive designations A: and B: are reserved for floppy disk drives. For years, this was the most common portable storage device. Most computers sold now do not come with floppy drives. USB flash drives have replaced floppy drives.

The C: drive is always the main internal drive in the computer. This is the drive on which the Win 7 software resides.

After the first three drive designations, the rules change a bit. You will see drives in various combinations and orders depending on how the computer is configured.

Internal drives get designated first, starting with hard drives, then CDs and DVDs.

Network drives are assigned next.

External drives are last and generally are assigned designations based on the order in which they are attached to the computer.

Behind the Screen *(continued)*

Numerous drives can be connected to your computer.

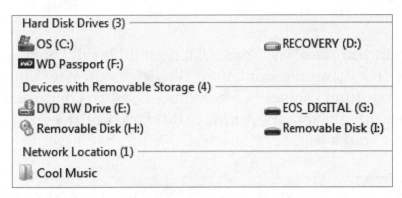

Example of a computer with seven drives connected and a network drive connection

 TIP! There are two important things to remember about drive letter assignments: The main internal drive in the computer will always be drive C:, but your USB flash drive *will not necessarily have the same letter designation* on every computer where it is used.

 HANDS-ON 4.1 **View Drives on Your Computer**

In this exercise, you will learn how to view the various drives on your computer.

1. Choose Start ⊕→Computer.

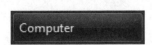

The Computer Explorer window appears. Notice the drives and drive letters on your computer.

2. Close ▓ **X** ▓ the Computer Explorer window.

Plugging In and Unplugging a Flash Drive

There is more to using a USB flash drive than inserting and removing it from a USB port on your computer. Your USB flash drive must be recognized by Win 7 when it is first plugged in and safely unplugged to avoid damage to data stored on the drive.

Plugging In and AutoPlay   Your USB flash drive can be plugged in to any USB port on a computer, but before you can use it, Win 7 must recognize the drive. Recognition can take a few moments; when completed, an AutoPlay dialog box usually appears. AutoPlay displays the drive name, its assigned drive letter, and a list of options available for that drive.

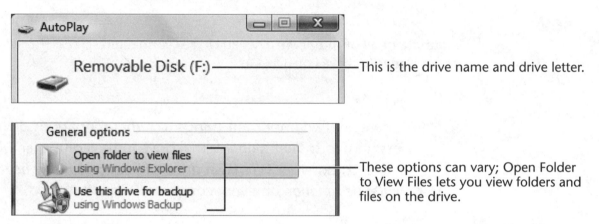

This is the drive name and drive letter.

These options can vary; Open Folder to View Files lets you view folders and files on the drive.

An AutoPlay dialog box

Unplugging Safely   Before you remove your USB flash drive, you must make sure Win 7 is no longer using the drive for any reason, such as saving a file. There is a risk of damaging the files on the USB flash drive if it is unplugged improperly. There are two primary methods to unplug a USB flash drive while the computer is running. (You can always safely unplug the drive after you properly shut down the computer.)

- **Activity light method:** If a USB flash drive has a blinking activity light, do not unplug the drive until a few seconds after the light stops blinking.

- **Safely Remove Hardware and Eject Media command:** If you want to be absolutely sure the drive can be unplugged safely, Win 7 provides the Safely Remove Hardware and Eject Media command. With this method, Win 7 notifies you when all activity on the USB flash drive stops and displays a prompt like the one below, letting you know that you can unplug it.

QUICK REFERENCE: Plugging In and Safely Unplugging a USB Flash Drive

Task	Procedure
Plug in a USB flash drive	• Insert your USB flash drive into any USB port.
	• When the USB flash drive has been recognized, an AutoPlay dialog box will appear.
Safely unplug a USB flash drive using the Safely Remove Hardware and Eject Media command	• Close all windows being used by the USB flash drive.
	• If necessary, click the Show Hidden Icons button on the Notification Area so all icons are visible.
	• Click the Safely Remove Hardware and Eject Media icon.
	• Choose the drive you wish to unplug from the list.
	• Wait for a Safe to Remove Hardware dialog box to tell you the device can be safely removed.
	• Unplug the drive.
Safely unplug using the activity light	• Close all windows being used by the USB flash drive.
	• Wait a few seconds after the activity light stops blinking and then unplug the device.

HANDS-ON 4.2 View Your USB Flash Drive

In this exercise, you will learn how to properly plug in your USB flash drive to the computer, open and close a file, and then safely unplug it.

1. Choose Start ⊞→Computer.

2. Insert your USB flash drive into an available USB port on the computer.

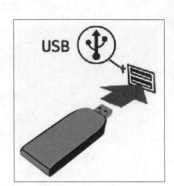

Once your drive is recognized, it will show up in the Computer Explorer window under the Devices with Removable Storage section, as shown in the following illustration. At this point, the USB flash drive is recognized and can be used like any other storage device on the computer. Take note of the name and drive letter because you will use these later in the exercise.

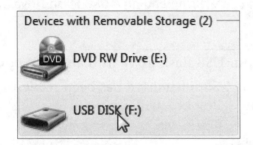

3. Close ▐ X ▐ the AutoPlay window if it appears. (You will explore the AutoPlay dialog box in Lesson 5, Storing Files).

4. Double-click to open your USB flash drive.

Win 7 displays the contents of the drive. If you used this drive in Lesson 3, Working with a Program, you should see the documents and Paint pictures you created in that lesson.

> ⚠ **NOTE!** In the next step, watch your USB flash drive immediately after you open the Memo to Ted Edwards file. You should see a small activity light flashing somewhere on the drive.

5. Double-click to open the Memo to Ted Edwards file.

The activity light on the USB flash drive flashes to indicate that it's performing some activity with the files on the drive.

Depending on the software installed on your computer, Win 7 launches WordPad, Word, or some other word processing program to display the file.

6. Tap [Enter] to insert a blank line in the document.

7. Close [x] the word processor window.

8. When prompted to save the file, click the Yes button.

The activity light flashes again. It's important to make sure that this light has stopped flashing before you unplug your USB flash drive (as you will do in a moment).

9. You can now safely unplug the USB flash drive from the computer.

Using Windows Explorer

Windows Explorer (or simply Explorer) is the Win 7 program that lets you view a computer's drives and the data on them. The following figure displays some key features of an Explorer window.

The address bar shows you where you are in the drive and folder system. In this example, you are viewing a USB flash drive. The address bar also lets you move around in the drive and folder system.

The Search box allows you to look for files and folders on your computer when you have forgotten their location or name.

The Folders pane lets you view all folders on all drives.

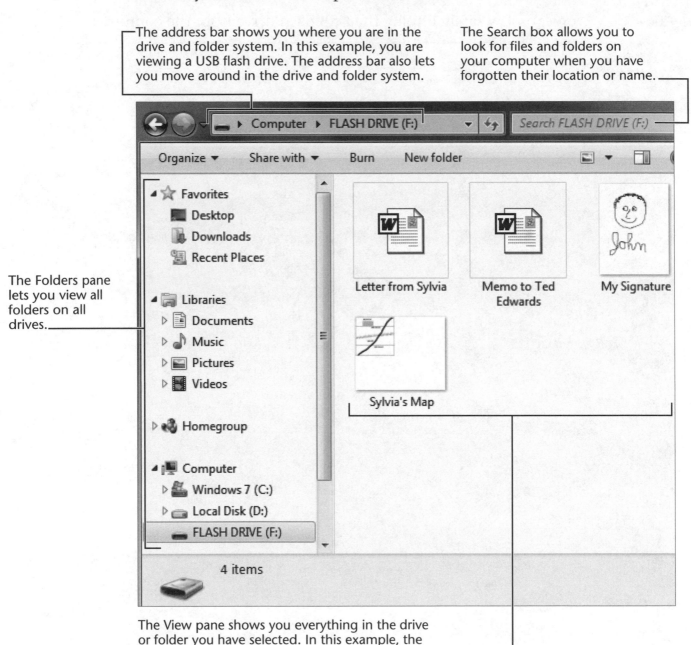

The View pane shows you everything in the drive or folder you have selected. In this example, the USB flash drive contains four documents.

!NOTE! Throughout the rest of this book, the Explorer window will be referred to as a folder window.

Common Folder Window Tasks

The folder window allows you to perform several useful tasks:

- **Browsing** for files and folders

- **Searching** for files and folders

- **Creating** new folders and using them to organize your documents

- **Renaming** files and folders

- **Moving and copying** files and folders

- **Deleting** files and folders

This lesson concentrates on the first two tasks. The other tasks will be covered in the next lesson.

> **!NOTE!** Don't confuse Windows Explorer with Internet Explorer. Windows Explorer is used to explore drives, folders, and files on your computer; Internet Explorer is a web browser used to explore the Internet.

Locating Personal Folders

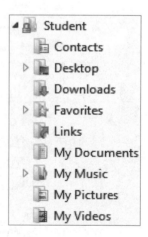

When a new login name is created, Win 7 creates a set of personal folders on the internal hard drive like the ones shown at right. These folders are intended to be the storage locations for that individual's folders and files. Because of their importance as a person's primary storage locations, Win 7 also provides quick access commands to these folders from various locations, such as the Start menu and folder windows. In the illustration, the login name is Student, so the main data folder also is given the name Student.

> **!TIP!** You can tell personal folders from normal folders because they have a custom graphic.

Locating Public Folders

Public folders are useful on machines where there are multiple users. Unlike personal folders, which are set up for each user, public folders are accessible by anyone on the computer.

These folders are useful if you have pictures or documents that need to be accessed by multiple people at home or at your office.

Navigating Your Drives and Folders

Being able to navigate drives and folders to locate your files is a critical skill. There are three easy-to-use navigation features built into the folder window:

- The address bar

- The Folders pane

- The Back and Forward buttons

Folders and Subfolders   Files are organized using folders. Folders can be further organized by adding more folders within them called subfolders. Any folder can have subfolders. This system is like having a filing cabinet drawer full of files organized in folders.

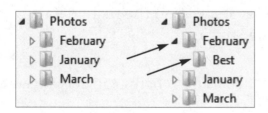

The Photos folder has a subfolder called February. The February folder also has a subfolder called Best.

The Address Bar

The address bar runs across the top of a folder window. The address bar displays a *path* (hierarchy) that includes a starting location and any drive, folders, or subfolders linked to the location currently open. The path is like a map with signs pointing to your present location. The path is Explorer's way of saying, "You are here, and this is how you got here." You can see how to navigate to your present location by following the path to the left.

This path (hierarchy) begins with the Computer folder on the left end of the path.

The folder you are currently viewing is the February folder at the right end of the path.

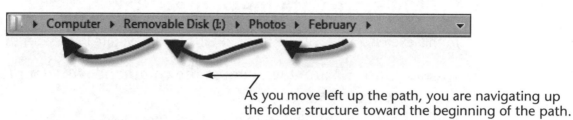

As you move left up the path, you are navigating up the folder structure toward the beginning of the path.

Navigating Via the Address Bar   The subfolders listed in the path actually are buttons that, when clicked, open that subfolder in the folder window. Each subfolder in the path also has a drop-down menu that shows its subfolders (accessed with the menu button ▸). The subfolders on the drop-down menu also display in the folder window if clicked. You are able to navigate (browse) the folder structure of the path using these subfolder buttons and drop-down menus.

Folder button   Menu button

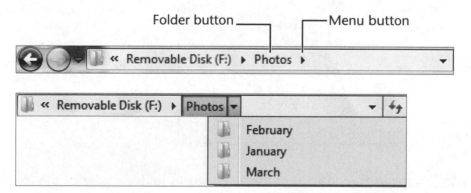

The menu ▸ button displays a list of subfolders in the Photos folder.

Task	Procedure	
Move to a different folder on the path	• Move your mouse pointer over a folder name on the path to see its button and click.	Photos ▼
Move to a subfolder in a folder on the path	• Move your mouse pointer over the menu ▶ button to see its button and click. • Click a subfolder on the drop-down list.	📁 January

 HANDS-ON 4.3 Navigate with the Address Bar

In this exercise, you will use the address bar to navigate in the user's folder.

1. Choose Start 🏵 and then choose the command with your login name at the top of the right pane.

   Win 7 opens a folder window to display the user's folder.

2. Follow these steps to navigate to the My Pictures folder:

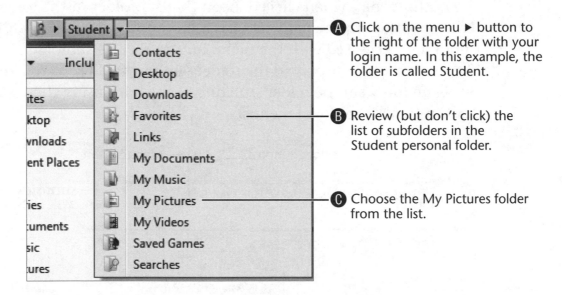

Ⓐ Click on the menu ▶ button to the right of the folder with your login name. In this example, the folder is called Student.

Ⓑ Review (but don't click) the list of subfolders in the Student personal folder.

Ⓒ Choose the My Pictures folder from the list.

Win 7 displays the content of the My Pictures folder and adds the folder name to the end of the address bar path.

3. Follow these steps to explore the default folders:

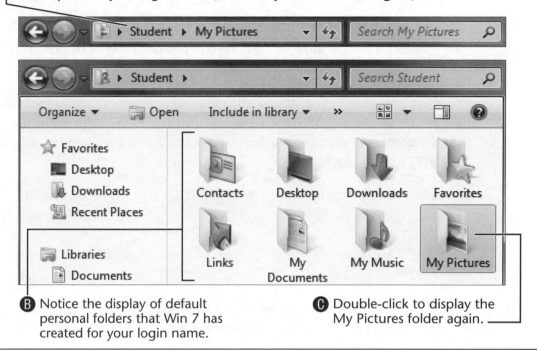

A Taking care not to click a menu ▸ button, click the name of the folder that represents your login name (which may not match this figure).

B Notice the display of default personal folders that Win 7 has created for your login name.

C Double-click to display the My Pictures folder again.

Using the Back and Forward Buttons

The Back and Forward buttons remember the order of the folders that you have viewed. If you choose to view a subfolder and then change your mind, the Back button will change your view back to your previous folder.

If you change your mind again, you can return to the subfolder you were just viewing by using the Forward button. The buttons work a lot like the back and forward buttons on a DVD remote control to move back and forth through the frames of a movie.

- The Back button takes you back to previously viewed locations in the reverse order of the way they were originally viewed.

- The Forward button doesn't work until you move back at least one step. (This is why that button is usually grayed out.)

!TIP! The Back and Forward buttons in Internet Explorer work just like the buttons in a folder window.

HANDS-ON 4.4 Practice with the Back and Forward Buttons

In this exercise, you will use the Back and Forward buttons in a folder window to navigate folders.

1. Choose Start →Pictures.

   Win 7 opens a folder window and displays the contents of the Pictures folder.

2. Double-click the Sample Pictures folder.

   The View pane (right panel) now displays the contents of the Sample Pictures folder. Notice that the Forward button is faded. This indicates that the button is inactive. The Forward button won't work until you use the Back button at least once.

3. Click the Back button to move back into the Pictures folder.

   Win 7 returns you to the previous view—in this case the Pictures folder. Notice that the Forward button is now colored, indicating that it is active.

4. Click the Forward button to return to the Sample Pictures folder.

   Win 7 moves you forward to the folder from which you had moved back, in this case back to the Sample Pictures folder.

5. Close the folder window.

Units of Measure for Computer Storage

Size and capacity in the computer world are based on the byte. A byte is the smallest unit of measurement in the computer world. When you are typing a letter, each character you type is one byte of information.

Measurement	Is Equal to...
Byte	1 character (e.g., *a*, *b*, *!*, etc.)
Kilobyte or "K"	1024 bytes
Megabyte or "meg"	1024 kilobytes
Gigabyte or "gig"	1024 megabytes
Terabyte	1024 gigabytes

 NOTE! This note is for math junkies only! Notice that all the numbers end in 24. Computer numbers tend to be based on factors of 8. To simplify these numbers, you often will see them rounded to the nearest thousand.

Common Data File Sizes   Different types of data that you create will require different amounts of storage space. A basic rule of thumb is that the more complicated the file, the more space it needs. A photo will need more space than a typed document; a home video will need more space than a photo.

Item	Approximate Size
Word processing document	20–30 kilobytes per page
Digital camera photo	1–7 megabytes, depending on your camera, the picture's quality, and its size
Music file	3–6 megabytes per song, depending on the audio quality and song length
Video file	1–20 megabytes for every 30 seconds, depending on the video's quality and format
HD video	1.7 megabytes per second or 50–55 megabytes per 30 seconds.

Changing the Folder View

The way folder and file information is displayed in the folder window can be changed using the View button or View options button. The View button can be clicked to cycle through eight different views. The option button can be used to display the eight view options.

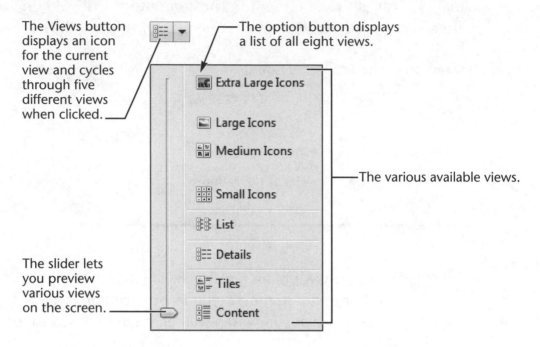

The Views button displays an icon for the current view and cycles through five different views when clicked.

The option button displays a list of all eight views.

The various available views.

The slider lets you preview various views on the screen.

As you work with files and folders, you may find that some views work better than others for various tasks.

 TIP! Folder and drive windows remember their view settings when closed. You may want to change the view as you complete the lesson exercises to more closely match the exercise figures.

Identifying the Contents of a Folder

The icons used to identify folders can tell you a lot about the kind of information stored in that folder. Win 7 changes the look of a folder icon (in certain views) to help you identify whether it holds subfolders or files and to indicate the file types. The folders will look different on each computer and change over time, depending on the files available in the folder to make the representations. The following table shows some of the common folder icons seen in Win 7.

Folder Type	Description	Folder Type	Description
 Basic Folder	This folder may be empty.	 Graphics	This folder contains only graphics and displays actual pictures.
 Multiple Files and Folders	When multiple file types are in the same folder, a generic folder like this is used.	 Documents	This folder contains documents. It may display program icons from Microsoft Office and other software.
 Music	This folder contains music; it displays album covers if available.	 Videos	This folder contains videos. It displays the first frame of a video or a program icon.

The Folders Pane

The Folders pane enables you to select files from a more complete view of the folder "tree" (hierarchy), starting with the Desktop. The Folders pane displays all the drives and folders on your computer, plus any attached external drives and their folders. When you click a folder, the contents of that folder are displayed in the View pane to the right of the Folders pane.

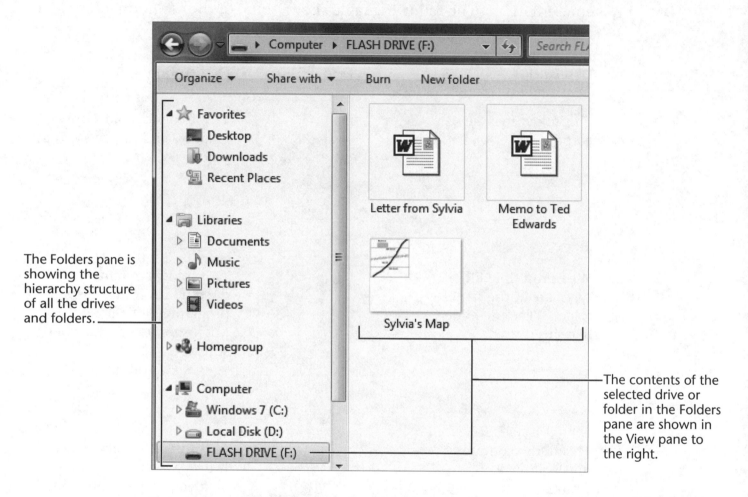

The Folders pane is showing the hierarchy structure of all the drives and folders.

The contents of the selected drive or folder in the Folders pane are shown in the View pane to the right.

Expanding Subfolders   Some folders may have an Expand View ▷ button on the left. The Expand View ▷ button enables you to see the subfolders in that folder. When clicked, the folder expands to show its subfolders without changing the view pane. When the triangular button is angled, it indicates that the folder is expanded.

The Expand View ▷ button shows that the folder has subfolders to view.

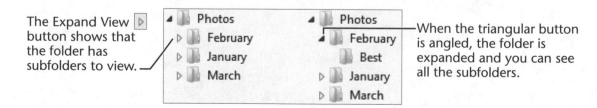

When the triangular button is angled, the folder is expanded and you can see all the subfolders.

HANDS-ON 4.5 **Navigate with the Folders Pane**

In this exercise, you will use the Folders pane in a folder window to navigate among folders.

1. Choose Start ⊕→Computer.

2. Maximize ▣ the Computer window.

3. Follow these steps to navigate with the Folders pane:

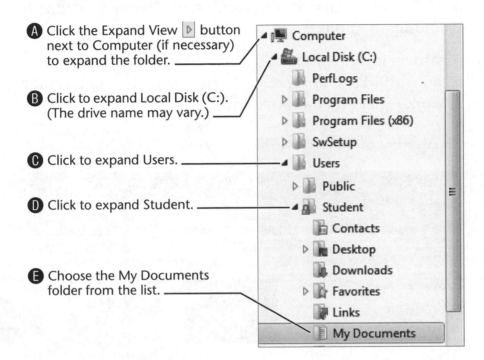

A Click the Expand View ▷ button next to Computer (if necessary) to expand the folder.

B Click to expand Local Disk (C:). (The drive name may vary.)

C Click to expand Users.

D Click to expand Student.

E Choose the My Documents folder from the list.

The View pane should now show the contents of the Documents folder. Depending on what others have done on the computer, there may or may not be many (or even any) items in this folder.

4. Choose the My Pictures folder in the Folders pane. (You may need to scroll down the list to make this folder visible.)

The View pane displays the contents of the My Pictures folder.

5. Close ▬ⓧ▬ the window.

Searching for Files

Win 7's Search command allows you to easily look for lost files or folders. By typing in part of a filename or some text from a document, Search displays (filters) the files and folders it finds that match your search text.

How Search Works

By default, Search automatically looks at files in the folder you are currently viewing, plus all of your personal folders, including Documents, Pictures, Music, and many more.

Win 7 gathers information about your various documents in the background while you work. This information is gathered into a large index that makes Search work faster and more accurately.

When you type one or more words in the Search box and tap [Enter]...

...Win 7 displays all files and folders related to your search text.

NOTE! Search may not seem important now, but as your music library grows or you start using a digital camera, the number of files in your personal folders may blossom into thousands. Without Search, finding lost files could become tedious.

QUICK REFERENCE: Searching for Files

Task	Procedure
Search for a file or folder	Type one or more search words in the Search box and tap ⟨Enter⟩.

HANDS-ON 4.6 **Find a File with Windows Search**

In this exercise, you will use Search to locate pictures in the Sample Pictures folder.

1. Choose Start 🪟 →Pictures.

   Win 7 displays the Pictures library folder, one of the default folders created in the Windows Library folder.

2. Double-click to open the Sample Pictures folder as shown at right.

   The Sample Pictures folder appears. Notice that this folder contains various pictures. Also, notice that the path to this folder is different. This path leads to a folder in the Libraries folder, rather than to a folder with your username.

Sample Pictures

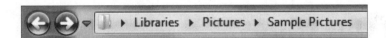

▸ Libraries ▸ Pictures ▸ Sample Pictures

3. Type **penguins** in the Search box.

▸ Search Results in Sample Pictures ▸ ▾ penguins ✕

Observe what is happening in the View pane. Win 7 is sorting through the sample pictures and leaving only the pictures that match your search request.

Win 7 will also display pictures if the search request matches "tags" or "keywords" that have been imbedded in the picture. None of the pictures have imbedded tags in the Sample Pictures folder.

Search Results in Sample Pictures

Penguins

4. Exit ✕ Search as shown to return to displaying all of the files in the Sample Pictures folder (not just the ones found by your search).

penguins ✕

Concepts Review

True/False Questions

1. You can securely remove a USB flash drive by simply unplugging it at any time.   **true**   **false**   _____

2. You can use Windows Search to find music and pictures as well as documents.   **true**   **false**   _____

3. Every login name has its own personal folders.   **true**   **false**   _____

4. USB flash drives are often called thumb drives.   **true**   **false**   _____

5. Folders can contain other folders (subfolders).   **true**   **false**   _____

6. Search will look for files only in the folder you are currently viewing.   **true**   **false**   _____

Multiple Choice Questions

1. My Documents, My Pictures, and My Music are examples of _____.
   Page number: _____
   a. media folders
   b. personal folders
   c. login folders
   d. search folders

2. How do you securely unplug a USB flash drive?
   Page number: _____
   a. Use the Safely Remove Hardware and Eject Media icon in the Notification Area.
   b. Close all open programs and gently remove it from the USB port once the Activity light stops blinking.
   c. Shut down the computer properly and remove it from the USB port.
   d. All of the above

3. In a folder window, you can navigate to various folders using _____.
   Page number: _____
   a. the address bar
   b. the Back and Forward buttons
   c. the Folders pane
   d. All of the above

4. A USB flash drive is a _____.
   Page number: _____
   a. a removable storage device
   b. an internal storage device
   c. a temporary storage device
   d. a network storage device

Skill Builders

SKILL BUILDER 4.1   Find the Remaining Capacity of a Drive

In this exercise, you will discover which folders and files are stored on your USB flash drive and how much space is left to store additional data.

Find What's Stored on Your USB Flash Drive

1. Plug your USB flash drive into a USB port on the computer.

   Depending on how it is configured, Win 7 probably will open an AutoPlay window asking what you want to do with the newly plugged-in drive.

2. Choose Open Folder to View Files from the bottom of the list. (You might need to scroll down to see this option.)

3. If an AutoPlay box does not appear after step 1, choose Start ⊕→ Computer and double-click on the USB flash drive icon to open it in a folder window; otherwise skip to step 4.

   Notice that a USB flash drive button has been added to the taskbar.

4. Open any folders on your USB flash drive to see what data has been stored, or continue with the next step if there aren't any folders on the drive.

   Are there any subfolders? What file types (data, photos, music) have you copied to the drive?

Find Out How Much Free Space Is Available

Now you will give a command to display the available space on your USB Flash drive.

5. Follow these steps to return to viewing the contents of your USB flash drive:

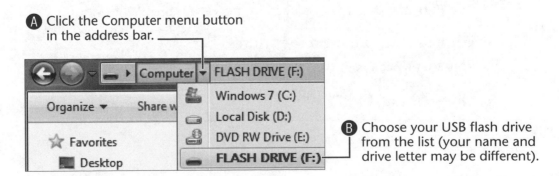

6. Right-click the USB flash drive icon and choose Properties.

Win 7 displays a pie chart and details about the storage space on your flash drive.

The Properties dialog box will show how much space is used and how much space is available for additional data.

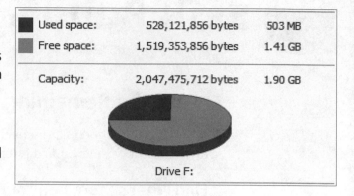

■	Used space:	528,121,856 bytes	503 MB
■	Free space:	1,519,353,856 bytes	1.41 GB
	Capacity:	2,047,475,712 bytes	1.90 GB

Drive F:

7. Click OK.

8. Close ⬛✕⬛ both windows.

SKILL BUILDER 4.2 View the Public Folders

In this exercise, you will learn how to find and view the Public folders from the address bar.

1. Choose Start ⊕→Computer.

2. Follow these steps to navigate to the Public folders:

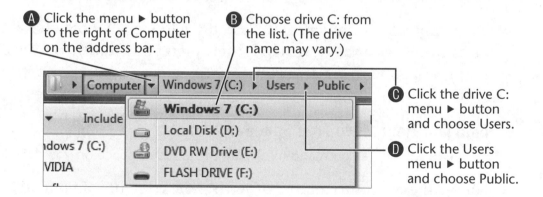

Ⓐ Click the menu ▶ button to the right of Computer on the address bar.

Ⓑ Choose drive C: from the list. (The drive name may vary.)

Ⓒ Click the drive C: menu ▶ button and choose Users.

Ⓓ Click the Users menu ▶ button and choose Public.

The Public folders are displayed in the View pane of the window.

3. Choose Computer on the address bar.

You are now back in the folder window that displays your drives.

4. Close ⬛✕⬛ the window.

Storing Files

At some point, after you have saved drawings from Paint and letters from WordPad or transferred pictures from your digital camera, you will want to organize these digital files. Win 7 provides methods to organize files that are similar to organizing a filing cabinet in an office. It provides folders and subfolders to group related items. Tools also are provided to move files from one folder to another, to make copies to put in other folders, and to delete unwanted files.

You also will want to make copies of your files to share and to create extra copies (backups) to protect against loss or damage to the files on your hard drive. You can copy digital files to portable storage devices including CDs, DVDs, USB flash drives, and external hard drives.

LESSON OBJECTIVES

After studying this lesson, you will be able to:

- Create new folders and subfolders to organize your files
- Move or copy folders and files from one location to another
- Delete folders and files and, if necessary, restore them from the Recycle Bin
- Organize your digital pictures
- Copy (burn) folders and files to CDs or DVDs

*Additional learning resources are available at **labpub.com/learn/silver/wtw7/***

Case Study: Getting Organized

Aileen has been creating and saving many different file types on her computer. She has lots of pictures from her digital camera, a small collection of her favorite songs, all kinds of homework from a half dozen classes—and a big mess. Her photos are stuffed into the Pictures folder like pictures thrown in a shoebox. Her music collection is okay, but she would like to put some of the songs on a CD to play in her car. Worst of all is her homework. It has all been saved in her Documents folder, but assignments from different classes are all mixed together. She wants all the homework from each class to be grouped together so she can easily find an assignment when she needs it.

Aileen has learned how to make subfolders. She decides to organize her personal folders the same way she would organize a filing cabinet. In Documents, she creates a subfolder for each semester, makes a subfolder for each class within the semester folders, and then moves the appropriate files into each folder. For her pictures, she creates folders marked with years and months in the Pictures folder. She also creates copies of pictures she used for homework and puts the copies into the class subfolders. Her folder system now looks like this:

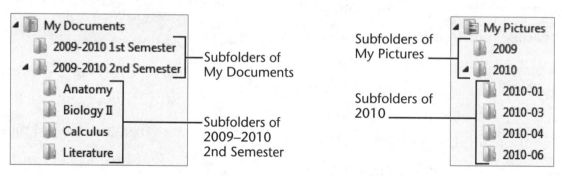

Aileen creates subfolders to organize her schoolwork and pictures.

Finally, Aileen is especially happy to notice the Burn button on the toolbar in Windows Media Player. She clicks the button and follows the instructions to copy her favorite music files to CDs. With Win 7, this is very easy to do.

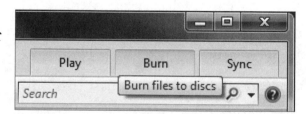

Creating Folders

The purpose of folders in the Win 7 system is to organize the thousands of files on your computer. Much like a filing cabinet in an office, folders enable you to organize files into groups—a folder for your Maui pictures or one for your science projects. Each person will have an individualized organizational style, but certain conventions must be followed as you create new folders:

- Folders can be created in another folder, on a drive, or on the Desktop.

- The naming conventions for folders are the same as those for naming files. Refer to the Naming Files Quick Reference table in Lesson 3. A folder name (including its entire path) can be up to 255 characters long and include some symbols, such as dashes, commas, ampersands, and apostrophes.

- You cannot have two folders with identical names in the same location. You will be asked if you want to replace the existing folder if you create a folder with the same name.

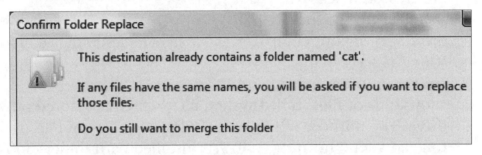

You will be warned if there are two folders (or two files) with the same name in the same destination (location) and be given the choice to merge or replace the existing folder with the new folder.

How Files Are Stored in Your Computer

There is an order to how your computer stores files on its various internal or external drives. The process for storing files is similar to procedures you might use to organize a filing cabinet. Individual documents, letters, or pictures (files) might be grouped together by subject, put inside folders, and labeled with an appropriate name. If there are many files within a folder, you might create subfolders to subdivide into more specific groups. The drives on a computer are organized in a similar manner using electronic folders, subfolders, and files.

Folders and Subfolders Created by Win 7

Electronic folders, subfolders, and files are created when Win 7 is installed on the local hard drive (C:) of your computer. Win 7 is a very large collection of programs with thousands of files, called system files, which are stored on your internal hard drive. The purpose of the system files is to carry out all of the tasks necessary to keep Win 7 running. Win 7 is installed with folders and subfolders to organize those system files and the files of other programs installed on your computer.

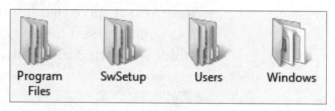

System folders installed on your local C: drive by Win 7.

Most of Win 7's system files are stored in a folder named Windows. The files in the Windows folder are grouped into several thousand subfolders.

When a new application program is installed onto your hard drive, some of the program files may be stored in the Windows folder, but the rest of the files are grouped into a folder with a name chosen by the manufacturer. This folder is then stored in the folder named Program Files.

As new users are added to your computer, a subfolder is created inside Win 7's Users folder with each user's name as a subfolder name. Win 7 also creates 11 personal subfolders for each user to organize his or her files: documents, pictures, music, videos, and other common types of files.

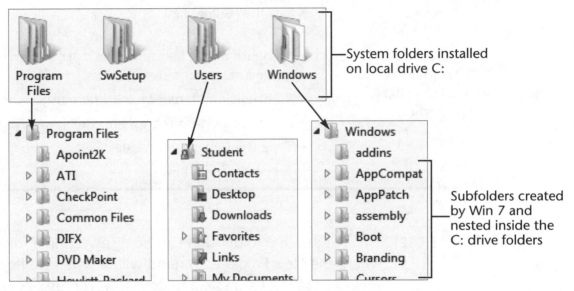

Thousands of folders and subfolders are created by Win 7 on your local hard drive.

Procedures for Creating New Folders

There are two commonly used procedures for creating new folders: using the New Folder button in the folder window and choosing from the right-click pop-up menu.

QUICK REFERENCE: Creating Folders

Task	Procedure
Create a new folder via the New Folder button	• Open the folder or the drive where you want to put a new folder. • Choose from the folder window toolbar. • Type the new folder name. • Tap the Enter key.
Create a new folder via the right-click method	• Navigate to the location (Desktop, folder, or drive) where you want to put a new folder. • Right-click a blank place in the window or on the Desktop. • From the pop-up menu, choose New→Folder. • Type the new folder name. • Tap the Enter key.

⚠ NOTE! The Desktop is a folder that can be displayed in a folder window, where the New Folder command will be available from the folder window toolbar to create a folder. However, usually you see the Desktop as your opening screen without menus, and you must use the right-click method to create a new folder.

Renaming Files or Folders

Sometimes you will want to correct or change the name of a file or folder and rename it. You must follow Win 7's naming conventions mentioned above when you rename a file or folder. You also can select and rename multiple files or folders at the same time. When you rename multiple folders, Win 7 will give one folder the new name—such as Maui—and the others will have the same name plus a serial number—Maui (2), Maui (3), Maui (4), and so on. When you rename multiple files, all files will be named serially starting with (1).

Task	Procedure
Rename files or folders from a toolbar menu	• Open the file or folder location. • Select one or more files or folders to be renamed. • Choose Organize→Rename from the toolbar. • Type the new name. • Tap the [Enter] key.
Rename files or folders using a right-click	• Open the file or folder location. • Select one or more files or folders to be renamed. • Right-click a selected item. • Choose Rename from the pop-up menu. • Type the new name. • Tap the [Enter] key.

HANDS-ON 5.1 Create a New Folder on the Desktop

In this exercise, you will create a new folder on the Desktop and give it a name. Then you will rename the folder.

Since there are no menus displayed on the Desktop for creating a folder, you will use the right-click method to display a pop-up menu, from which you can create one.

Create and Name a New Folder

1. Follow these steps to create a new folder on the Desktop:

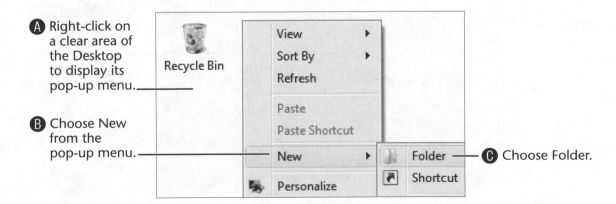

Ⓐ Right-click on a clear area of the Desktop to display its pop-up menu.

Ⓑ Choose New from the pop-up menu.

Ⓒ Choose Folder.

The new folder appears with its name selected, ready for you to type a new one.

2. To name the folder, type **Practice** and tap [Enter].

Rename the Folder

3. Right-click the Practice folder.

4. From the pop-up menu, choose Rename.

5. Type the new name **Delete Practice** and tap ⌊Enter⌋.

This folder will be used in Hands-On 5.6.

Creating Subfolders

When a folder gets filled with files, you may want to divide the files into groups using subfolders. Those subfolders could have their own subfolders, and so on. Subfolders are also called *nested* folders. When a new login name, such as Student, is created, Win 7 creates a personal folder named Student along with 11 subfolders (including My Documents, My Pictures, My Music) that are nested inside. If you then nest two subfolders named Animals and Flowers inside the My Pictures folder, the *path* (hierarchy) would look like this:

The address bar path shows that you are currently viewing the My Pictures folder.

The My Pictures folder has two folders nested inside, as displayed in the View pane.

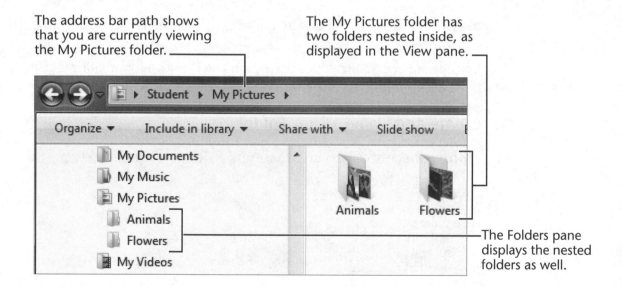

The Folders pane displays the nested folders as well.

HANDS-ON 5.2 Create Folders on Your Flash Drive

In this exercise, you will create two new folders on your USB flash drive.

Navigate to Your USB Flash Drive

1. Connect your USB flash drive to a USB port.

Wait a moment for the computer to recognize the USB flash drive. Depending on your USB flash drive and system setup, an AutoPlay dialog box should appear. (If AutoPlay does not appear, skip to step 3.)

The AutoPlay box displays the drive name and its assigned drive letter and provides a list of options available for that drive. (The name and drive letter you see will probably differ from the one shown at right.)

2. Choose Open Folder to View Files from the AutoPlay list (you may have to scroll down to see this option) and then skip to the Create a New Folder section of this exercise.

3. Choose Start ⊕→Computer and double-click on the icon for your USB flash drive if AutoPlay did not appear in step 1.

Create a New Folder

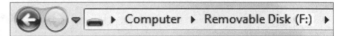

Win 7 displays the contents of your USB flash drive. Notice the drive name and letter in the path of the address bar. (The name and drive letter you see will probably differ from the one shown at right.)

Now that you have navigated to your USB flash drive, you are ready to create folders on it. The New Folder command always creates the new folder at your current location.

4. Follow these steps to create and name a new folder:

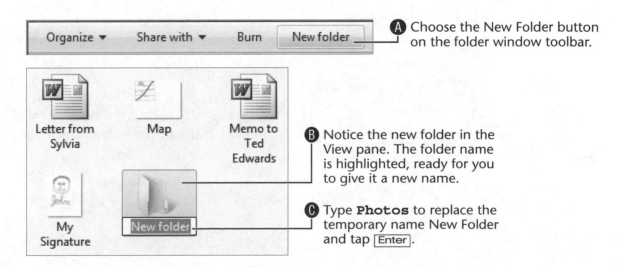

Ⓐ Choose the New Folder button on the folder window toolbar.

Ⓑ Notice the new folder in the View pane. The folder name is highlighted, ready for you to give it a new name.

Ⓒ Type **Photos** to replace the temporary name New Folder and tap Enter.

5. Double-click the new Photos folder to open it.

The folder is empty, so nothing displays in the View pane.

6. Click the Back  button.

The View pane displays the contents of your USB flash drive. The Photos folder has moved to the top of the list. Win 7 normally displays folders before any files.

Create an Additional Folder

7. Choose the New folder button from the folder window toolbar.

8. Name the new folder **USB Documents** and tap the Enter key.

The two new folders on your USB flash drive will be used in the following exercises.

Moving and Copying Folders and Files

From time to time you may want to reorganize your folders and files. You can easily move folders and files to a new location or put copies of folders or files in other locations.

Using the Cut, Copy, and Paste Method

To cut and paste or copy and paste folders and files, you use methods similar to those used for text and objects in Lesson 3, Working with a Program. Take time to compare the similarities and differences. As with text, you must select at least one folder or file before you can give the Cut or Copy command. You will learn how to select more than one folder or file at a time later in this lesson.

The Cut, Copy, and Paste commands are conveniently located in the Organize menu on the folder window toolbar.

How the Commands Work

The following applies to folders and files being cut or copied and pasted within a folder window:

- **Cut:** Deletes a selected file or folder from its present location only *after* a copy of that file or folder is pasted into a new location.

- **Copy:** Leaves a selected file or folder in its present location when it is pasted into a new location.

- **Paste:** Inserts (into the folder or drive currently open) a copy of the last file or folder that was cut or copied.

- **Undo:** Undoes your most recent Paste command.

More About the Paste Command   A few additional features of the Paste command are useful to know:

- You can paste only once if you cut a file or folder.

- You can paste more than once if you copy a file or folder.

- You can usually use the Undo command if you paste into a wrong location.

QUICK REFERENCE: Managing Folders and Files with Cut, Copy, and Paste

Task	Procedure
Move folders or files with Cut and Paste	• Select the folder or file you want to move. • Choose Organize→Cut from the folder window toolbar. • Move to the new location (the Desktop, a folder, or a drive). • Choose Organize→Paste from the folder window bar.
Copy folders or files with Copy and Paste	• Select the folder or file you want to copy. • Choose Organize→Copy from the folder window toolbar. • Move to the new location (the Desktop, a folder, or a drive). • Choose Organize→Paste from the folder window toolbar.
Undo a Paste command	• Immediately after pasting in error, choose Organize→Undo from the folder window bar.

HANDS-ON 5.3 **Organize Folders with Cut, Copy, and Paste**

In this exercise, you will copy a file and place the copy into a different location using Copy and Paste and then move a file using Cut and Paste.

Before You Begin: You will be using folders created in Hands-On 5.2 and files created on your USB flash drive in Lesson 3, Working with a Program. Your USB flash drive should already be connected.

Copy and Paste Method

1. Navigate to your USB flash drive, choose Start ⊕→Computer→USB Storage Device (or whatever your USB flash drive is named; this can vary).

2. Follow these steps to copy a file into a folder:

Ⓐ Click the Letter from Sylvia to select it and then choose Organize→Copy from the folder window toolbar.

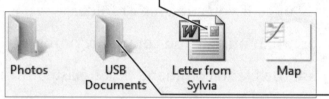

Ⓑ Double-click the USB Documents folder to open it and then choose Organize→Paste from the folder window toolbar.

3. Click the Back ⊕ button on the toolbar.

Win 7 moves you out of the folder, back to viewing your USB flash drive again. The original Letter from Sylvia file is still on the drive.

4. Double-click the USB Document folder to open it again.

5. Choose Organize→Undo from the folder window toolbar to remove the copied file.

6. From the Delete File prompt that appears, choose Yes.

The copied file disappears because the Copy command has been undone. If you make a mistake moving or copying files, you can usually (but not always) undo it.

7. Click the Back ⊕ button on the toolbar to view your USB flash drive window.

The original Letter from Sylvia file is still on the drive.

Cut and Paste Method

8. Follow these steps to move a file into a folder:

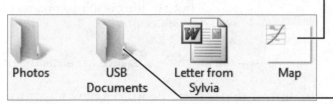

Ⓐ Click the Map file to select it and then choose Organize→Cut from the folder window toolbar.

Ⓑ Double-click the USB Documents folder to open it and then choose Organize→Paste from the folder window toolbar.

9. Click the Back Ⓖ button on the toolbar to return to the drive window.

The Map file is no longer on the drive; it has been moved.

10. Choose Organize→Undo from the folder window toolbar to return the moved file.

The Map file is returned to the drive because the Cut command has been undone.

Drag and Drop Method

You used drag and drop in Lesson 1, Getting Your First Look to move cards in Solitaire. Folders and files in the same location can be easily moved or copied using the drag and drop method.

Win 7 has a great feature when you drag and drop a folder or file onto another folder or different drive. If you hesitate over the new location, a ScreenTip displays the default action (Move or Copy) and the name of the folder or drive where the object is being dropped.

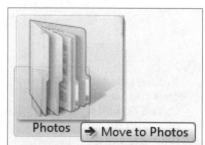

Although the left mouse can be used to drag, it is better for new users to use the right mouse button when dragging and dropping folders and files. The right mouse button gives you more control over what will happen when you drop the folder or file. Using the right mouse button displays a menu when you release the button. From that menu, you then get to choose a command to complete the procedure.

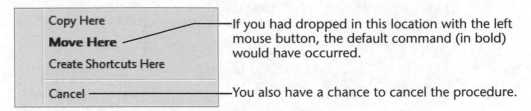

Copy Here	
Move Here	— If you had dropped in this location with the left mouse button, the default command (in bold) would have occurred.
Create Shortcuts Here	
Cancel	— You also have a chance to cancel the procedure.

Using the right mouse button to drag and drop to a new location lets you choose Copy Here or Move Here from a pop-up menu.

> **TIP!** Develop a good habit. Because you have more control over the procedure and are less likely to make mistakes, use the right mouse button to drag and drop.

 HANDS-ON 5.4   Copy and Move Files Using Drag and Drop

In this exercise, you will use your right mouse button with drag and drop to copy and move a file to another location.

Copy Files with Drag and Drop

1. Follow these steps to move and copy files using the drag and drop method and the right mouse button:

Ⓐ Place your mouse pointer over the Memo to Ted Edwards file, hold down with the right (not the left) mouse button and drag over the USB Documents folder, and release the mouse button.

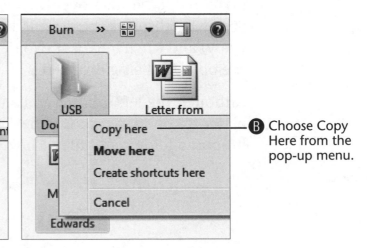

Ⓑ Choose Copy Here from the pop-up menu.

The Memo to Ted Edwards file is still on the drive window.

2. Double-click to open the USB Documents folder.

Notice that a copy of the Memo to Ted Edwards file is now in the folder.

3. Choose Organize→Undo from the folder window toolbar.

4. From the Delete File prompt that appears, choose Yes.

The document disappears because the Copy command was undone.

5. Click the Back [⬅] button.

Move a File Using Drag and Drop

6. Using the right mouse button, drag the My Signature file onto the USB Documents folder and release the mouse button.

The pop-up menu appears, asking what you want to do with the file.

7. Choose Move Here from the pop-up menu.

The My Signature file disappears from view because it has been moved into a folder.

8. Double-click the USB Documents folder to open it.

The My Signature file is there, as you would expect.

9. Click the Back [⬅] button.

10. Choose Organize→Undo from the folder window toolbar.

The My Signature file reappears in the USB flash drive view because the Cut command was undone.

Selecting Multiple Files

You can select more than one folder or file at a time. When you select multiple folders or files, Win 7 lets you move or copy the whole group at the same time. To select multiple folders or files, you can use the Ctrl key or Shift key with mouse clicks. You also can drag a selection box with the mouse to select a group of folders or files.

QUICK REFERENCE: Selecting Multiple Folders and Files

Task	Procedure
Select multiple contiguous folders or files	• Click on the first folder or file. • Hold down the Shift key, click the last folder or file in the group, and then release the Shift key. *Note:* You can add additional folders or files to the selection by holding down the Ctrl key and clicking on the items you wish to add.
Select multiple noncontiguous folders or files	• Hold down the Ctrl key and then click once on each folder or file you wish to select. *Note:* Click a selected item while holding down the Ctrl key to deselect it.
Select a group of folders or files by dragging	• Taking care not to point at any file or folder, place the tip of the mouse pointer below the last file or folder in the group of files or folders you wish to select. • Drag with the left mouse button up and to the left to make a selection box large enough to select the group.
Selecting all folders and files	• Choose Organize→Select All from the folder window toolbar. *or* • Hold down the Ctrl key and tap the A key.

FROM THE KEYBOARD

Ctrl+A to select all

HANDS-ON 5.5 **Select and Move Multiple Items**

In this exercise, you will select multiple items by clicking while holding down the $\boxed{\text{Ctrl}}$ or $\boxed{\text{Shift}}$ keys and then by dragging a selection box. Finally, you will move a group of files using a right mouse button drag and drop.

Select Multiple Items by Clicking

1. Follow these steps to select multiple items using the $\boxed{\text{Shift}}$ key:

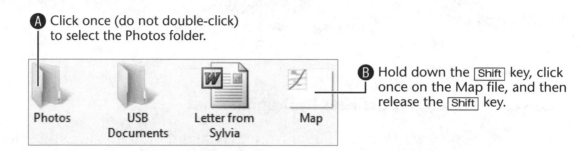

Ⓐ Click once (do not double-click) to select the Photos folder.

Ⓑ Hold down the $\boxed{\text{Shift}}$ key, click once on the Map file, and then release the $\boxed{\text{Shift}}$ key.

Notice that using the $\boxed{\text{Shift}}$ key selected the contiguous folders and files between the first and last selected items.

2. Follow these steps to select multiple items using the $\boxed{\text{Ctrl}}$ key:

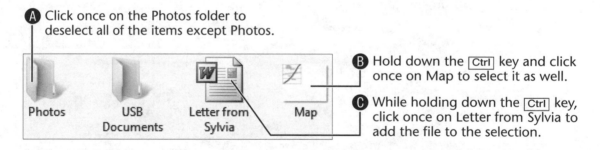

Ⓐ Click once on the Photos folder to deselect all of the items except Photos.

Ⓑ Hold down the $\boxed{\text{Ctrl}}$ key and click once on Map to select it as well.

Ⓒ While holding down the $\boxed{\text{Ctrl}}$ key, click once on Letter from Sylvia to add the file to the selection.

Notice that using the $\boxed{\text{Ctrl}}$ key lets you select noncontiguous items.

You also can combine the $\boxed{\text{Shift}}$ and $\boxed{\text{Ctrl}}$ key methods to select several files with $\boxed{\text{Shift}}$ and then select or deselect other folders and files with $\boxed{\text{Ctrl}}$.

Select Multiple Items by Dragging

3. Follow these steps to select multiple items:

Ⓐ Place the mouse pointer under the Map file, hold down the left mouse button, and drag a selection box that touches the icons for the Map and the Letter from Sylvia files.

Ⓑ Release the mouse button and notice that both files remain selected.

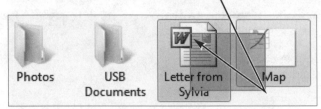

Move Multiple Files by Dragging

4. Make sure that the Letter from Sylvia and Map files are still selected and then follow these steps to move the multiple selected files:

Ⓐ Hold your mouse pointer over one of the selected icons (Letter from Sylvia or Map), hold down the right mouse button, and drag the files over the USB Documents folder (notice the ScreenTip).

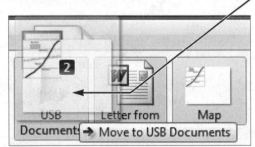

Ⓑ Release the mouse button and choose Move Here from the pop-up menu.

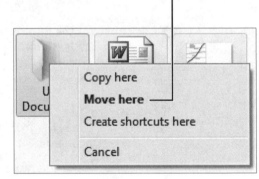

The files disappear from view as they are moved into the folder.

5. Double-click the USB Documents folder to open it and confirm that the files have been moved.

6. Close ▇ X ▇ the folder window.

Deleting and Restoring Folders and Files

Win 7 enables you to clean up your computer folders by deleting unwanted folders and files. Folders and files that are deleted from an internal or external hard drive are moved to the Recycle Bin folder. Folders and files in the Recycle Bin can later be returned to their original locations if desired.

The Recycle Bin

The Recycle Bin is a unique folder and important enough that Win 7 puts an icon linked to the Recycle Bin folder on the Desktop. The Recycle Bin folder serves as a temporary storage place for folders and files deleted from internal hard disk drives.

It is like a recycle bin you might have at home. When you put something into a recycle bin, it stays there unless you change your mind and retrieve it, or until it is permanently removed by the recycling truck. Likewise, folders and files sent to the Recycle Bin folder can be retrieved and sent back to their original locations (restored), but a folder or file that is deleted from the Recycle Bin is permanently deleted.

!WARNING! If you right-click on the Recycle Bin icon on the Desktop and choose Empty Recycle Bin, all of its folders and files will be permanently deleted.

Deleting Folders and Files

Not all deleted folders and files are moved to the Recycle Bin. Only folders and files deleted from drives categorized by Win 7 as hard disk drives are moved to the Recycle Bin. Folders and files deleted from drives categorized by Win 7 as devices with removable storage (such as USB flash drives and CD/DVD drives) are not moved to the Recycle Bin. These deleted folders and files are permanently deleted and cannot be restored.

Deleting Folders and Files from Hard Disk Drives   Folders and files are moved to the Recycle Bin when you delete them from your hard drive or other external devices recognized as hard disk drives. Win 7 displays a Delete dialog box similar to the illustration below if the deleted objects will be moved to the Recycle Bin:

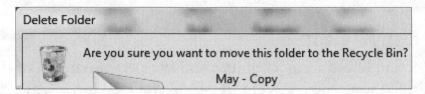

This Delete dialog box indicates that the folder will be moved to the Recycle Bin.

Deleting Folders and Files from Removable Storage   When you delete folders or files from a removable storage device such as most USB flash drives, they are permanently deleted without being moved to the Recycle Bin and cannot be restored. Win 7 will display a Delete dialog box similar to the following illustration if the deleted objects will not be sent to the Recycle Bin.

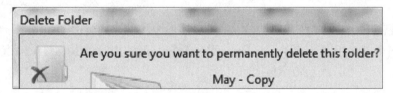

This Delete dialog box indicates that the folder will be permanently deleted instead of being moved to the Recycle Bin.

 NOTE!   USB flash drives normally show up as removable drives. Occasionally, some will show up as hard drives. As a precaution, you should always assume that folders and files deleted from USB drives will be permanently deleted.

Restoring Folders and Files

Deleted folders and files moved to the Recycle Bin folder can be restored (moved back) to the original locations from which they were deleted. When the Recycle Bin is opened, there is a Restore All Items button on the toolbar of the folder window. The Restore command button is used to initiate the restore, but its label will change depending on the number of items selected:

Restore all items	Restore this item	Restore the selected items
No items selected	One item selected	More than one item selected

QUICK REFERENCE: Deleting and Restoring Folders and Files

Task	Procedure
Delete a file or folder	• Select one or more folders and/or files you wish to delete. • Tap the Delete key on the keyboard. • Choose Yes to confirm the deletion.
Open the Recycle Bin	• Double-click the Recycle Bin icon.
Restore items from the Recycle Bin	• Open the Recycle Bin. • If desired, select one or more items to be restored, using the Ctrl or Shift keys if necessary. • Click the Restore button on the toolbar. 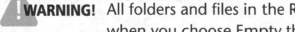
Empty the Recycle Bin	• Double-click the Recycle Bin icon to open it. • Click the Empty the Recycle Bin button on the toolbar.

> **⚠ WARNING!** All folders and files in the Recycle Bin are permanently deleted when you choose Empty the Recycle Bin.

HANDS-ON 5.6 **Delete and Restore Folders or Files**

In this exercise, you will delete a folder on the Desktop and then restore it. Use the folder named Delete Practice you created in Hands-On 5.1.

Before You Begin: Your USB flash drive should be displayed in a folder window. If necessary, repeat steps 1 and 2 of Hands-On 5.2 to display this drive.

Delete a Folder

1. Click the Delete Practice folder on the Desktop to select it.

2. Tap the ⌑Delete⌑ key to delete it.

   Win 7 asks, "Are sure you want to move this folder to the Recycle Bin?" This confirms that it will be moved to the Recycle Bin rather than permanently deleted.

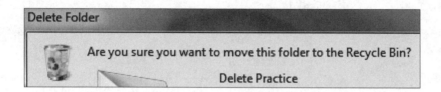

3. Choose Yes to confirm the move to the Recycle Bin.

Restore the Folder

4. Double-click the Recycle Bin icon on the Desktop.

   Win 7 opens a new folder window to display the contents of the Recycle Bin. Depending on what others have done on this computer, it may contain just the folder you deleted or many other folders and files as well.

5. Find the Delete Practice folder in the Recycle Bin and click to select it. (You may need to scroll down the list. Or you can tap the letter ⌑D⌑ on the keyboard to jump directly to the first item—alphabetically—with a name that starts with D.)

6. Click the Restore This Item button on the folder window toolbar.

   Restore this item

7. Close ▧X▧ the Recycle Bin and confirm that the Delete Practice folder is restored to the Desktop.

Organizing Digital Pictures and Videos

As digital cameras have found their way into homes, large numbers of picture and video files have found their way onto to computers. Organizing your digital pictures and videos is essential, or you will end up with the digital equivalent of a large cardboard box jammed with pictures. Without organization, finding your digital pictures and videos becomes time-consuming and frustrating. Win 7 provides several ways to organize pictures and videos, and many other companies offer picture organizer (catalog) programs.

Via Folders

One simple way to organize your digital pictures and videos is to use Win 7 folders and subfolders to group related pictures. In previous exercises you learned to create, copy, and move files and folders. It is important to pick a folder system that seems logical to you and will enable you to easily find a picture or video a month from now or a year from now. Example folder structures include the following:

- Folders for each year with subfolders named for each month

- Folders for each year with subfolders named for events during the year, such as Maui Vacation, Mike's Birthday Party, or Jane's Wedding

- Folders grouping general topics, such as Vacations with subfolders named 2008 Maui, 2009 Grand Canyon, or 2010 Toronto

!NOTE! Try This at Home 5.1 at the end of this lesson gives guided practice in organizing pictures via folders on your own computer.

Via Windows Photo Gallery

Microsoft has a website called Windows Live Essentials, where additional software can be downloaded without cost. Photo Gallery is a Live Essentials program that helps you view and organize your pictures and videos.

Photo Gallery can work with any Win 7 folder structure you decide to use, but it also lets you filter and view pictures using the following criteria:

Criterion	Result
All Pictures and Videos	Lets you scroll through all pictures and videos in multiple folders without having to open each one
Tags	Lets you add tags (keywords) to pictures and then filter pictures using the tags
Date Taken	Lets you filter pictures by the date and time the picture was taken by a camera or scanned on a scanner
Ratings	Lets you add a rating of one to five stars to pictures and videos and filter them by their star ratings
Folders	Lets you scroll through pictures and videos in selected folders without having to open each folder

Via Organizer and Album Programs

There are dozens of photo organizer and album (catalog) programs available. Many digital cameras include album and editing software, and you can access web-based album-sharing services or download free organizing software. Other organizer and album programs offer features similar to Photo Gallery but may be packaged with additional features such as more advanced editing software.

 Check the website for this book for links to some popular photo album, organizer, and catalog programs.

Burning CDs and DVDs

When you burn a CD or DVD, there should be no smoke. *Burn* means to copy (write) files onto to a disc. People burn CDs and DVDs for three purposes:

- To transport folders and files to other computers or devices

- To back up (archive) their folders and files

- To share their folders and files with others

Most Win 7 computers come with a combo DVD/CD burner (drive) that can record both DVDs and CDs, though some burners may record only CDs. Win 7 has simplified the burning process by providing Burn buttons in various programs, including Explorer and Media Player.

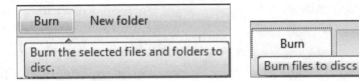

Burn buttons and ScreenTips look different in Explorer and Media Player.

About CD/DVD Media

CDs and DVDs look alike, but they are quite different. In Lesson 4, Finding Files, you learned that CDs can store about 700 MB of data, but DVDs can store about 4,700 MB and more. A DVD player can play DVDs and often CDs, but a CD player cannot play DVDs. You also should be aware of CD/DVD types, as outlined in the following table.

CD or DVD Type	Stands For	Capabilities
R	Recordable	• Write files, but do not erase them. • Very suitable for long-term storage of files.
RW	Rewriteable	• Write, erase, and rewrite files. • Not suitable for long-term storage of files.
ROM	Read Only Memory	• Read files, but do not write them. • Commercial CDs are in this format.
DVD+, DVD–	Plus or Minus	• Competing DVD formats, both available in R, RW, and ROM. • Used for high-volume data storage and movies.

 **WARNING!** When using a pen to label a CD or DVD, use only soft-tipped pens designed to mark CDs and DVDs and do not press hard. Ink with solvents or using too much pressure can damage the data stored on your CDs and DVDs.

Win 7's CD/DVD Burning Utility

Win 7's built-in burning utility lets you copy data, pictures, or videos. Before you begin burning, make sure you have the correct disc type for your CD/DVD burner. The Burn a Disc dialog box lets you name the disc and choose one of two formats, as outlined in the following table.

Format	Options	Purpose
Live File System	Like a USB flash drive	This format lets you add and erase data on the disc, much like a USB flash drive. Discs can be read only by Win XP, Win Vista, and Win 7.
Mastered	With a CD/DVD player	You must copy all of the files at the same time. In addition to Win XP, Win Vista, and Win 7, discs can be read by Windows versions before Win XP, as well as by some ordinary CD and DVD players.

The Burning Process The process of burning files to a disc can be much slower than copying files to a USB flash drive. When burning files to a new disc, Win 7 must first format the disc, and only then can it copy the files. Ejecting a disc also can take a few moments because Win 7 must close the current session and prepare the disc to be used on other computers. Win 7 will display the following notification balloon:

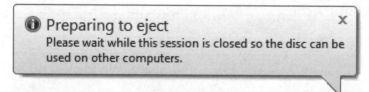

Before you can eject a CD or DVD, a balloon informs you that Win 7 must properly close the session.

Third-Party CD-Burning Utilities

There are other CD-/DVD-burning programs available with enhancements beyond the basic burning tools built into Win 7. Some computer manufacturers include alternative burning software with their computers.

 Check the website for this book for links to other burning programs.

 HANDS-ON 5.7 **Create a Data Disc with Win 7**

In this exercise, you will burn a data disc using the built-in burning utility.

Before You Begin: Yo*u will need a new (blank) CD, and your USB flash drive should be plugged in.*

 A web-based simulation of this exercise is available in case you do not have a recordable CD. Follow these instructions to use the WebSim:

1. Open your web browser, enter **labpub.com/learn/silver/wtw7/** in the address bar, and tap the Enter key.

2. Click the Hands-On 5.7: Create a Data Disc with Win 7 link.

3. Tap the F11 key on the keyboard to display the full screen view (if necessary).

   Now you can follow the instructions below to "burn" a CD via the simulation. If a step for the simulation differs at all from the following instructions, an onscreen note will appear.

4. Click the Start button to simulate placing a CD in the CD burner.

   An AutoPlay window may appear, asking what you wish to do with the CD.

5. Close ██X██ the AutoPlay window if it appears.

6. Choose Start ⊕→Computer.

   Win 7 opens a window to display all the drives on your computer. If necessary, scroll down the drive list and then double-click your USB flash drive icon to view its contents.

7. Follow these steps to start the burning process:

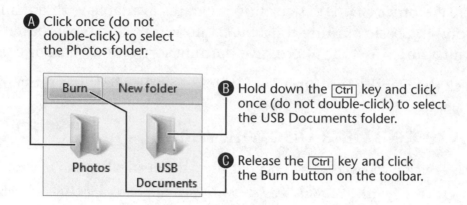

A Click once (do not double-click) to select the Photos folder.

Burn | New folder

Photos | USB Documents

B Hold down the Ctrl key and click once (do not double-click) to select the USB Documents folder.

C Release the Ctrl key and click the Burn button on the toolbar.

After the disc is scanned, the Burn a Disc dialog box appears, ready to guide you through the steps of burning a CD.

8. Follow these steps to tell Win 7 how to burn the CD:

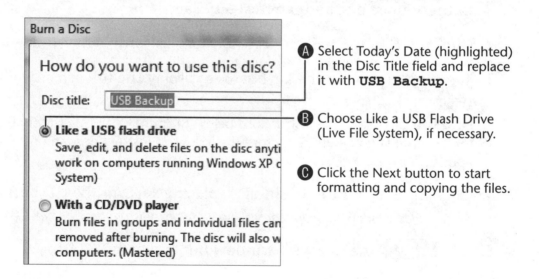

Burn a Disc

How do you want to use this disc?

Disc title: USB Backup

○ **Like a USB flash drive**
Save, edit, and delete files on the disc anyti work on computers running Windows XP c System)

○ **With a CD/DVD player**
Burn files in groups and individual files can removed after burning. The disc will also w computers. (Mastered)

A Select Today's Date (highlighted) in the Disc Title field and replace it with **USB Backup**.

B Choose Like a USB Flash Drive (Live File System), if necessary.

C Click the Next button to start formatting and copying the files.

While Win 7 is burning, a prompt will appear estimating the time the burn will take, and then the burner drive will open in a drive window to show folders being added to the drive.

9. When the burn has finished, double-click the USB Documents folder in the CD folder window to confirm that the files also have been copied.

10. Close ▬ X ▬ both windows.

Concepts Review

True/False Questions

Page number

1. The rules for naming folders are the same as those for naming files.　　**true**　**false**　_____

2. You can use the Cut and Paste commands to move folders and files from one location to another.　　**true**　**false**　_____

3. Deleted folders and files are always moved to the Recycle Bin.　　**true**　**false**　_____

4. If you delete a picture from the Desktop and then restore it, Win 7 restores it to the My Pictures folder.　　**true**　**false**　_____

5. Folders and files deleted from a USB flash drive are not placed in the Recycle Bin.　　**true**　**false**　_____

6. Burning to a CD/DVD is slower than copying to USB flash drive.　　**true**　**false**　_____

Multiple Choice Questions

1. You can create new folders _____.

   Page number: _____
   a. in an existing folder
   b. on a drive
   c. on the Desktop
   d. All of the above

2. On which type of CD can you write but not rewrite?

   Page number: _____
   a. CD-R
   b. CD-RW
   c. CD-ROM
   d. None of the above

3. Multiple files and folders can be selected by _____.

   Page number: _____
   a. clicking with the Shift key held
   b. clicking with the Ctrl key held
   c. dragging across files and folders
   d. All of the above

4. One advantage of using a DVD instead of a CD is that a DVD _____.

   Page number: _____
   a. does not scratch as easily as a CD
   b. is not damaged by solvent-based pens like CDs
   c. can hold much more data than a CD
   d. None of the above

Skill Builders

SKILL BUILDER 5.1 Find and Copy Files

In this exercise, you will find Win 7's sample images on the computer and copy eight of them to a new folder on your USB flash drive.

View Your USB Flash Drive

1. Plug your USB flash drive into a USB port on the computer.

2. When the AutoPlay box appears, choose Open Folder to View Files (you may have to scroll).

   The Windows Explorer button has become active on the taskbar. If an AutoPlay box does not appear, choose Start→Computer and double-click on the USB flash drive icon to open the drive in a folder window.

Copy Pictures

3. Open the Pictures library folder with Start ⊕ →Pictures.

4. Double-click Sample Pictures, if available, or follow these step to open the Sample Pictures folder from the Folders pane:

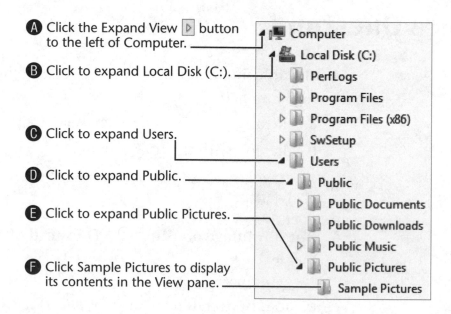

Ⓐ Click the Expand View ▷ button to the left of Computer.

Ⓑ Click to expand Local Disk (C:).

Ⓒ Click to expand Users.

Ⓓ Click to expand Public.

Ⓔ Click to expand Public Pictures.

Ⓕ Click Sample Pictures to display its contents in the View pane.

△ ▣ Computer
 ▲ 💾 Local Disk (C:)
     📁 PerfLogs
   ▷ 📁 Program Files
   ▷ 📁 Program Files (x86)
   ▷ 📁 SwSetup
   ▲ 📁 Users
     ▲ 📁 Public
       ▷ 📁 Public Documents
         📁 Public Downloads
       ▷ 📁 Public Music
       ▲ 📁 Public Pictures
           📁 Sample Pictures

5. While holding down the ⌈Ctrl⌋ key, click eight pictures of your choice in the View pane to select them; release the ⌈Ctrl⌋ key after you've made your selections.

6. Choose Organize→Copy from the folder window toolbar to copy the group of eight pictures to the Clipboard.

Create a New Folder and Paste the Pictures

Pasting a large a group of pictures or other data onto your USB flash drive can create clutter. You can create a new folder on the USB flash drive for the group first, give it an appropriate name, and then open the new folder before you paste the group.

7. On the taskbar, click the button for your USB flash drive window to make it active.

8. Choose New folder from the folder window toolbar to create a new folder. Name the new folder **Copied Photos** and tap ⌈Enter⌋.

You can perform other tasks (such as creating a new folder) between giving the Copy and Paste commands because copies of the eight pictures remain in Clipboard.

9. Open the new Copied Photos folder.

Before you choose the Paste command, you must be located in the destination folder.

10. Choose Organize→Paste from the folder window toolbar to copy the group of eight pictures into the folder.

There should be some small versions (thumbnails) of the pictures you copied showing within the Copied Photos folder.

11. Click the drop-down arrow to the right of the ▤ ▼ button on the toolbar and choose Extra Large Icons.

12. Click the Back ⊙ button to return to the display of the USB flash drive.

When you choose a new view, it affects only the location you are in when you choose it.

13. Click the drop-down arrow to the right of the ▤ ▼ button on the toolbar and choose Extra Large Icons again.

14. Close ⌈ X ⌋ the folder window.

Try This at Home

TRY THIS AT HOME 5.1 **Create Folders and Organize Pictures**

In this exercise, you will find a folder with pictures, create subfolders to group pictures together by subject, and copy the pictures into the subfolders. Finally, you will rename the pictures in each folder.

Before You Begin: If you have your own pictures at home that you need to organize, open their location and use those. If you have no pictures of your own, use Win 7's Sample Pictures.

1. Open the Pictures library folder with Start→Pictures.

   If you are unsure about where your pictures have been stored, review the folders and files displayed here.

2. If you do not have pictures of your own, double-click Sample Pictures, if available, or follow these step to open the Sample Pictures folder from the Folders pane:

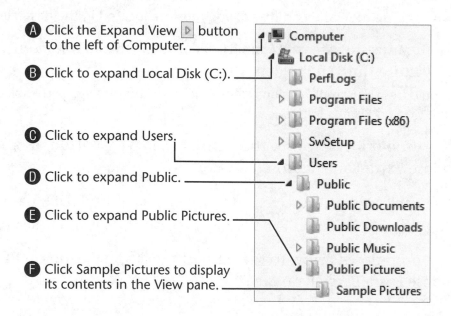

Ⓐ Click the Expand View ▷ button to the left of Computer.

Ⓑ Click to expand Local Disk (C:).

Ⓒ Click to expand Users.

Ⓓ Click to expand Public.

Ⓔ Click to expand Public Pictures.

Ⓕ Click Sample Pictures to display its contents in the View pane.

Create a New Folder

3. Open the location where your pictures are stored in a folder window.

4. Determine different subjects for the pictures and create a new folder for each subject using the New Folder button from the folder window toolbar.

   In the Sample Pictures folder, you might create folders named Plants, Animals, and Water.

5. While holding down the ⎡Ctrl⎤ key, click pictures to select a group that you want to move or copy to an appropriate new folder.

Clicking with the ⎡Ctrl⎤ key held down selects or deselects pictures when creating groups that you want to move or copy into a folder.

6. Use the right mouse button to drag and drop the group of pictures onto the appropriate folder. When you release the right mouse button (drop), choose Copy Here from the pop-up menu.

Some pictures fit into two or more subjects (such as a whale or a turtle in the water). Those pictures can be copied to more than one folder.

7. Repeat steps 5 and 6 to select groups of pictures and copy them into each subject folder.

Rename the Files

8. Double-click to open the first subject folder, hold down the ⎡Ctrl⎤ key, and tap ⎡A⎤ to select all of the pictures in the folder.

9. Right-click on one of the selected pictures and choose Rename from the pop-up menu.

10. Type their subject name (such as *Trees*) and tap ⎡Enter⎤.

Pictures will have the subject name Trees plus a serial number: Trees (1), Trees (2), Trees (3). Renaming pictures can be particularly useful when pictures are named with only a serial number assigned by a camera.

11. Repeat steps 8–10 to rename the pictures in each subject folder with their subject name.

 TIP! From now on, these new folder and picture names can be used to locate (filter) these pictures by typing the names in the Search command of your user folder or in other organizers.

Beyond the Basics

In this unit, you will begin by connecting to the Internet. You will find that the Internet allows you to access information, pictures, movies, music, games, and much more. Then you will learn how to change certain looks and features associated with Win 7 using the Control Panel. Finally, you will work with Win 7's Help and Support features so you know how to locate assistance on the tasks you want to perform.

Using the Internet

Connecting to the Internet has become one of the primary reasons for owning a computer and learning to use computer technology. The Internet provides you with access to a wealth of information on almost any topic; entertainment with pictures, movies, music, and games; and the ability to shop the world from home. In this lesson, you will use Internet Explorer to browse the web.

LESSON OBJECTIVES

After studying this lesson, you will be able to:

- Use a World Wide Web address to surf directly to a website
- Identify the main components of a web address
- Use Internet Explorer to browse the web
- Create a favorite with Internet Explorer
- Perform a basic Google search on a specific topic

*Additional learning resources are available at **labpub.com/learn/silver/wtw7/***

Case Study: Researching on the Web

Patrick is planning a trip to Arizona and figures most of the information he needs is available

on the Internet. He starts his search in Internet Explorer by typing *grand canyon* in the Instant Search box that is to the right of the address bar.

Sometimes when he searches there seems to be too much information, and he needs to narrow the search by trying different words. Fortunately, the first page has two perfect links: a link to Grand Canyon pictures and one to the official National Park Service site for the Grand Canyon (www.nps.gov/grca).

A link to the National Park Service site for the Grand Canyon ——

A link to pictures of the Grand Canyon

The web address (URL) for the web page ——

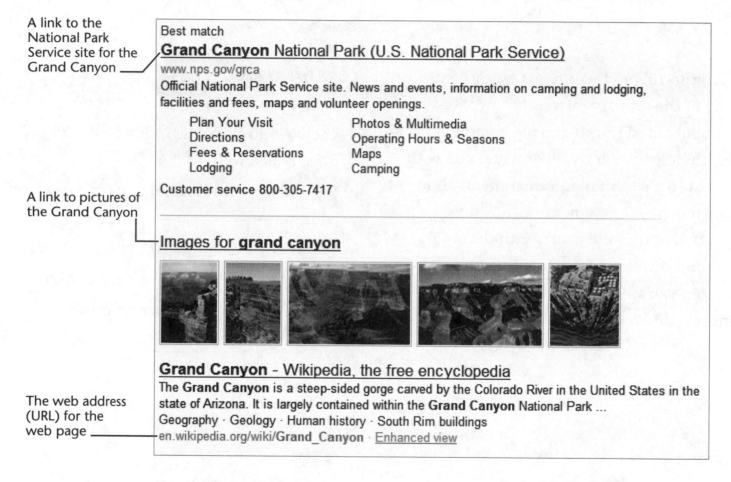

The National Park Service web page has everything Patrick needs: hotels, restaurants, events, and things to do. There are links to make reservations, helpful information, maps, and beautiful pictures. This site is going to make planning his trip easier, so he adds the web page to his favorites.

Introducing the Internet

The Internet has been in existence for more than 40 years. In its infancy, it was text-based and was used primarily by the military and educational institutions. Using the Internet often involved typing long strings of text on a black screen (see the illustration below). That changed in the early 1990s with the creation of the World Wide Web. The World Wide Web simplified access to information through a graphical interface that included colored graphics and point-and-click links. Users didn't have to remember and type complex addresses or know specifically where information was located; they could just point and click on links or onscreen buttons to jump to the information. This made the Internet easier to use, more colorful, and more interesting.

This is Victoria Free-Net accessed using an older, text-based technology (Telnet, top left) and with a newer graphical browser technology (Internet Explorer, bottom right).

The World Wide Web

By far the most dominant segment of the Internet is the World Wide Web (WWW), commonly referred to as the *web*. The web is only one of many technology pieces that make up the Internet, but it has become the most commonly used because of its simplicity and graphical features.

Today's web pages have colorful multimedia displays and easy-to-click links to other web pages. Most people can access the web by learning some simple skills and understanding a few basic concepts.

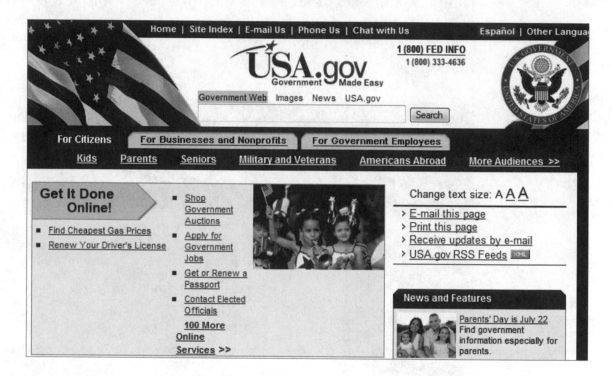

Equipment Used to Connect to the Internet

You need specific equipment to connect to the Internet. New computers typically include most of the equipment needed, but some equipment may be provided to you by your Internet service provider (ISP).

Dial-Up Modems   A *modem* (stands for **mod**ulate/**dem**odulate) enables your computer to connect to the Internet via a standard telephone line. The dial-up modem converts the analog signals of the phone system into the digital signal your computer uses. Once connected to a phone line, your computer can dial the phone number of your ISP to gain access to the Internet. Dial-up modem connections are slow compared to the high-speed connection options available in most parts of the country today.

Dial-up modem connection on the back of a computer. Your phone line can plug directly into the computer.

High-Speed Modems   A high-speed modem converts the signals sent over telephone lines, over cable lines, or from a satellite into signals your computer can use to communicate with the Internet. It is called a high-speed modem because it moves data to and from your computer at a much faster rate than a conventional dial-up modem.

Routers   Once you have an Internet connection, a router enables you to connect multiple computers in your home to that connection. A typical router will allow four computers to be networked together with network cable so that they can all access the Internet.

Wireless Routers   A wireless router works just like a regular router with the added benefit of allowing access to the Internet via a wireless connection. Most laptop computers now have wireless capability. They can connect wirelessly at home or from other locations that make their wireless routers available to the public, such as coffee shops, restaurants, and hotels.

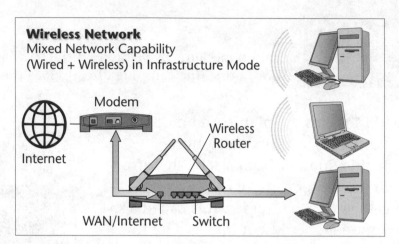

Wireless Network
Mixed Network Capability
(Wired + Wireless) in Infrastructure Mode

Modem

Internet

Wireless
Router

WAN/Internet   Switch

In infrastructure mode, a router or access point handles all network traffic.

 NOTE!   There are other specialized ways to connect to the Internet, and new technologies are emerging all the time. The way Internet service is delivered keeps changing with the advent of Internet over power lines or WiMAX. The way the service is used also keeps changing, with the development of more portable devices. The Internet now can be accessed through cell phones and laptops, but it might someday be built into your sunglasses or wristwatch.

Connection Types

Connection to the Internet is made possible through a business known as an ISP. Connecting to a service provider can be accomplished in several different ways:

• Via telephone line using a dial-up modem

• Via telephone line using a high-speed modem (DSL)

• Via TV cable using a high-speed modem

• Via a network at work or school

• Via wireless connections, such as satellites, cell towers, and dish systems

Internet Service Providers   An ISP provides the connection between you and the Internet. The ISP is usually paid a monthly fee to maintain your connection to the Internet. Many ISPs provide other services as well, and they might provide Internet services as part of a bundle of multiple services. Your ISP might be a company that specializes in Internet connections, but it might also be your phone service company or cable/satellite TV service company.

In most cases, the ISP will provide you with software that will automatically configure your computer with the correct settings for your new Internet connection and instructions for setting up any needed equipment.

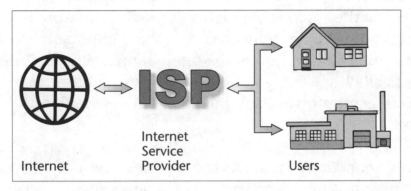

To access the Internet, you must first connect to an ISP.

Dial-Up Connections   A dial-up connection was the first type of Internet connection available to home consumers. A dial-up connection uses a dial-up modem and a standard phone line (sometimes referred to as POTS, for plain old telephone system).

Dial-up gets its name from the fact that special software in your computer has to dial a phone number to make the connection. On some computers you can actually hear the modem make touch-tone-like sounds as it dials the ISP's telephone number as well as various screeching tones as it "handshakes," or establishes a connection with, the ISP's computers.

Dial-up connections are the slowest type of Internet connection. They are widely available in the United States because they use existing phone lines, and the fee charged for dial-up service is commonly lower than for other types of Internet connections.

High-Speed Connections   *High-speed* is a generic term for services that provide information transfer rates that are higher than typical dial-up transfer rates. You can access high-speed connections through your TV cable, phone line (referred to as digital subscriber line, or DSL), or even satellite dish.

High-speed connections can be more than 50 times faster than dial-up connections. A document that would take you 20 minutes to download over a dial-up connection might take only a few seconds with a high-speed connection.

Network Connections   When you use a computer at work or school, you are connected to the Internet through a network. A network is a group of computers connected together that can share information and services such as the Internet. Connection to the Internet on a network is designed to move more data at a higher speed (more *bandwidth*) and to share that information with many computers at the same time. The Internet itself is a network of networks.

Wireless Connections   Wireless connections have become popular for an obvious reason—there is no wire. That means you do not have to be tied to a desk. You can be mobile and still be connected to the Internet. Typically, wireless connections are slower than some other high-speed connections but still much faster than dial-up connections.

Connection Speeds   Connections are measured in kilobits per second. High-speed connections may reference their speed in megabits. One megabit equals 1,000 kilobits.

Connection type	Speed	Example
Dial-up connection	56 kilobits	• 5–7 seconds to view an average web page • 20–30 minutes to download one song
High-speed connection	256–2,000 kilobits	• 1–2 seconds to view an average web page • 30–45 seconds to download a song • Less than one hour to download a movie

Web Browsers

Once you're connected to the web, you need a web browser to explore it. The web is like a very large coffee table book—millions of pages filled with vibrant pictures, text, and sounds on any topic you can think of. The browser lets you explore this "book," jumping from page to page using special text and graphics that link you to other pages.

Internet Explorer   The exercises in this lesson use Internet Explorer, which is Microsoft's popular and widely used browser. It comes installed with all versions of Win 7. Internet Explorer is the dominant browser in the today's market, but there are competing browsers.

Internet
Explorer

Other Browsers

- **Firefox:** One of the most popular alternatives, Firefox is a free browser that you can download and use on your Win 7 computer. Firefox is available at www.mozilla.com.

Firefox

- **Chrome:** One of the newest browsers available, Chrome was created by Google and is very popular among Google fans. Chrome is available at www.google.com/chrome.

Google
Chrome

There are dozens of other browsers available on the Internet. One of the great features of the Internet is the ability to explore and discover many new pieces of software and various ways to accomplish the digital tasks you need to complete.

America Online   America Online (AOL) is a unique service on the World Wide Web. America Online not only connects you to the web but also provides many services and resources itself. If you think of the web as a city, AOL would be like a gated community within that city. You can get a variety of services in the vast metropolis of the web, but you get specialized services within the gated community overseen by AOL.

AOL 9.0

HANDS-ON 6.1 **Start a Web Browser**

In this exercise, you will start Internet Explorer, the default web browser on most Win 7 computers.

1. Click the Internet Explorer icon located to the right of the Start button.

After a pause, an Internet Explorer window opens to display a web page. Briefly review the page content and notice the layout of the window.

Leave the window open to use in the next exercise.

Understanding Universal Resource Locators (URLs)

In order for a browser to find specific sites, there needs to be a way to uniquely identify them. Every site on the Internet has a Universal Resource Locator, or URL. A URL is also referred to as an address. You use the address to find and display a particular website (location). It's similar to finding a house by looking for its unique address, and just like houses, no two websites can have the same address.

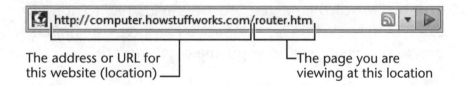

The address or URL for
this website (location)

The page you are
viewing at this location

Top-Level Domains   Website addresses are divided into major *domains*. The original domains were used to break Internet addresses into groups of websites with a common purpose. These six domains are used mainly by American websites, because the U.S. government was their creator and manager. As the web has gotten more popular, more and more foreign websites are using these major domains because of their global commercial success. The domain appears at the end of a web address.

The domain *.com* appears at the end of this URL.

Here are the original top-level domains:

- **.com:** Short for commercial. This is the most commonly used domain. It is open to any business, organization, or individual.

- **.edu:** Short for education. This domain is reserved for the use of educational institutions, such as schools and colleges. There are special requirements for groups wanting to use an .edu domain.

- **.gov:** Short for government. Federal, state, and local government websites will have this ending. When surfing the web, seeing the .gov domain ensures that the information you are looking at is official government information, something that can be hard to tell with some .com websites.

- **.org:** Short for organization. This top-level domain was once reserved for nonprofit organizations, but today anybody can register for .org names.

- **.net:** In times past, the .net domain was used mostly for Internet-related companies, but as businesses have had trouble finding good web addresses ending in .com, they have turned to .net domains.

- **.mil:** Short for military. One of the least used domains on the Internet. This top-level domain is reserved for the American military to use. Why does the military get their own top-level domain? The early research that created the Internet was funded by ARPA.

A complete list of top-level domains, including recently added domains, can be found at http://en.wikipedia.org/wiki/List_of_Internet_top-level_domains.

Country Codes Country codes also are top-level domains and consist of two-letter abbreviations that appear at the end of an address. Every country in the world has been assigned a country code that can be used in the creation of web addresses.

This web address ends in .ca, which is the country code for Canada.

Although addresses with country codes are not as common, you will find more of them as you research outside commercial and American websites.

Country	Code	Country	Code
United States	.us	Canada	.ca
England	.uk	Japan	.jp
Mexico	.mx	France	.fr
Iraq	.iq	Russia	.ru
Antarctica	.aq	Cuba	.cu

 A link to a complete listing of country codes is on the web page for this book.

Basic Navigation

Let's explore how Internet Explorer enables you to navigate the web. With some basic buttons and commands, you can move from location to location.

- **The address bar:** The address bar is where you enter the address of a web page or website.

- **Back and Forward buttons:** The Back button takes you back to previously viewed web pages while the Forward button returns you to more recently viewed web pages.

- **Refresh button:** Some web pages have content that changes frequently (such as an auction site). The Refresh button enables you to reload the page without having to type the address in the address bar again.

- **Stop button:** This button stops a page from loading. If a web page is taking too long to load, clicking the Stop button will stop the loading process. This enables you to type in a new address or click the Refresh button to try loading the page again.

Back and Forward buttons ____

The address bar ____

The Refresh button ____

The Stop Button

Hyperlinks

A *hyperlink*, or "link," is text or a picture that is linked to another page on the web. If you think of the web as a giant book, these links allow you to jump from one page to another in the book.

Typically, text links will be underlined and blue in color. On occasion, you will find text links that are colored other than blue.

Picture links can look like a normal image or be designed to look like buttons.

When your mouse cursor is over a picture or text link, it will turn into a small hand with a pointing finger. When you click the mouse, you will be taken to whatever page that link points to.

Once you reach a web page or a website, you can move to other web pages or other websites (or the websites' other pages) by clicking the hyperlinks.

DNA Test Indicates Very Green Greenland
WASH_GTON (AP) - Ice-covered Greenland rea
forests in a climate much like that of Sweden a
recovered ancient DNA from the bottom of an i

Japan May Have Oldest Right Whale Fossil
TOKYO (AP) - Researchers at a museum in cen
years old, making them the oldest fossilized rem
working in Nagano prefecture (state) estimate

When your mouse pointer is over a link in a web page, the pointer turns into a small hand, indicating that it is a link.

 HANDS-ON 6.2 **Navigate to a Web Page**

In this exercise, you will enter the address for Google News and use the Back button to navigate.

Before You Begin: Internet Explorer should be open from the last exercise.

1. Click in the address bar, type **news.google.com** as shown at right, and tap the Enter key.

   Notice that Internet Explorer automatically adds *http://* at the beginning of the address. This is required for the address to be valid. Most browsers now enter that part of the address for you.

2. Use the Back button on Internet Explorer to go back to the start page of your browser.

Tabbed Browsing

One of the features in Internet Explorer is tabbed browsing. This feature enables you to have multiple web pages open at the same time. Each web page has a tab (like a recipe card) making it easy to flip through your open web pages.

This feature comes in handy when you are doing research because you can have multiple sources open at the same time and quickly jump back and forth among them by clicking the tabs. It is also a great way to scan news headlines because it enables you to have multiple newspaper websites opened simultaneously.

TIP! Tabbed browsing is particularly useful when your Internet connection is running slowly. As one page is loading, you can be reading another.

The busy symbol appears while the web page is loading into your browser. Even with a high-speed Internet connection, you may have to wait for a page to load because of congestion on the web or the popularity of a website.

This image shows Internet Explorer with three web pages open on different tabs. The first web page is still loading and displays the system busy symbol. While it's connecting, you could be reading the news from one of the other tabs.

 HANDS-ON 6.3 Use Tabbed Browsing

In this exercise, you will open two pages within Internet Explorer. Internet Explorer should be open from the last exercise.

1. Click in the address bar, type **news.google.com**, and tap the Enter key.

2. Click the small New Tab box to the right of the larger tab labeled Google News.

A new What Do You Want to Do Next tab is created, and information about tabs is displayed in the viewing area.

3. Click in the address bar, type **cnn.com**, and tap the Enter key.

Internet Explorer opens the CNN homepage and displays the name in the new web page tab. You should now have two tabs open.

4. Position your mouse cursor over the Google News tab and click.

You jump back to Google News.

5. Position your mouse cursor back over the CNN.com news tab and click.

The browser's view switches back to CNN.

6. Position your mouse cursor back over the Google News tab and click.

7. Click on the Google News tab. Click the red X on the tab when it appears, as shown at right.

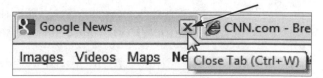

The Google News tab closes while the CNN tab remains displayed. Leave Internet Explorer open to use in the next exercise.

Favorites

A *favorite* is a link to a web page that you save in your browser. A favorite makes it easy for you to return to a web page in the future. Internet Explorer gives you the ability to remember numerous addresses in its list of favorites.

When you make a website a favorite, you do not have to remember its address or accurately type it in the address bar every time you want to visit the site. You simply access it from the Favorites Center.

Favorites Center The Favorites Center is a gathering spot in Internet Explorer for favorites you have created while surfing the web.

From here you can access any favorite you have saved, read any news feeds you have set up (an advanced feature not discussed in this book) and view a history of websites you have visited (Internet Explorer automatically creates the history list).

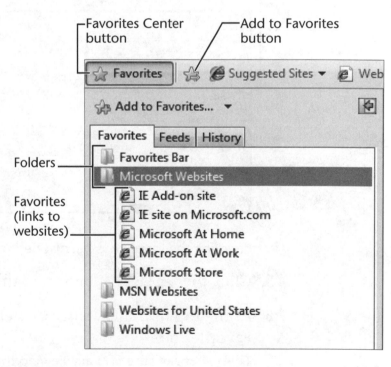

 TIP! Not all browsers use the term "favorites." Some browsers, such as Firefox, use the term "bookmark" instead.

FROM THE KEYBOARD

Ctrl + D to add a web page to your favorites

Alt + C to view your favorites

HANDS-ON 6.4 **Create a Favorite**

In this exercise, you will create a favorite in Internet Explorer. Internet Explorer should be open from the last exercise.

1. Click in the address bar, type **google.com**, and tap the ⌑Enter⌑ key.

2. Click the 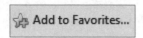 button.

3. Choose Add to Favorites from the drop-down menu that appears.

⭐ Add to Favorites...

4. Use the following steps to name your favorite:

Ⓐ The default name is selected; if necessary type **Google** to replace it. The default name may not always be descriptive enough and can be changed.

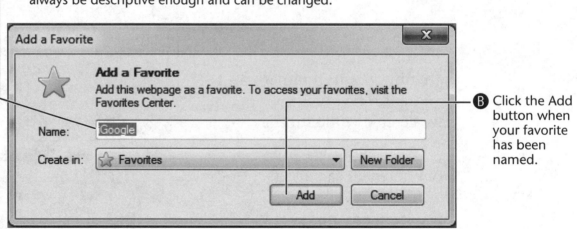

Ⓑ Click the Add button when your favorite has been named.

Your link to Google has been added to the Favorites Center.

5. Click the ⭐ Favorites button to the left of the tabs.

6. At the top of the Favorites Center pane, click the Favorites tab.

This will make sure you are viewing the Favorites Center and not one of the other options.

7. Find the Google favorite you created and click it.

You may have to scroll down to find it. Unless you choose a different location, Internet Explorer adds new favorites to the bottom of the list.

The Google web page linked to the favorite will be displayed in the View pane.

8. Close ![X] Internet Explorer.

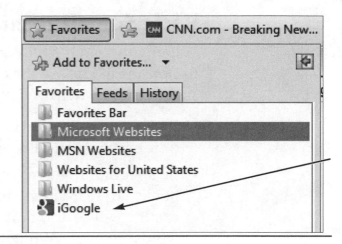

Performing a Basic Web Search

Finding information on the web is easy if you know where the information is located and you have a web address (URL) already. When you don't know its location, finding information can be more difficult. Luckily, there are tools called *search engines* that can help you search and find the information you want from the millions of pages that make up the web.

Search engines are specialized websites that help you find and sort information on the web. Think of a search engine as your own personal web librarian.

How Search Engines Work

Search engines, such as Google, index the web. This is similar to the way Win 7 indexes the information on your computer and then uses that index when you use the Search command in a folder window.

Google indexes the web using a vast network of computers around the world that index, or "crawl," the web every few days. When you perform a search, the search engine will create a list of the most relevant web pages it has indexed based on your search words.

Basic Search Techniques

When you search for information on the web using a search engine, it is important to choose the correct words to describe an item. Here are some suggestions to help you with your searching:

- **Pick a few keywords to describe your search item.** In most cases, three or four words should be enough.

- **Be specific.** If you are interested in books about Win 7, using "computer books" to search will display millions of possible web pages, or "hits," but the list will be too broad. You can narrow your search with more specific words, such as "Windows 7 books." This will bring up a shorter list of web pages that are more relevant.

- **Spell your search words correctly.** Misspelled words will generate a list, but it is not likely to be useful.

- **Keep trying.** If you are not finding what you are looking for, add and remove words from your search. Try different words. Even on the web, some subjects can be difficult to find information on. For example, if you are trying to find information on stabilizing riverbanks, "stabilize" and "bank" would be difficult words to use in a search, because you would tend to get mostly financial news related to banking issues. You could try using words such as "stream," "restoration," or "erosion" with the word "river." Sometimes when searching, the quickest way to an answer is not the most obvious.

 HANDS-ON 6.5 Search with Google

 In this exercise, you will perform a basic search with google.com. Because the web changes so frequently, this exercise runs as a simulation.

1. Use Start ⊞ →Internet Explorer to start the web browser.

2. Type **labpub.com/learn/silver/wtw7/** in the address bar and tap the ⸢Enter⸣ key.

3. Click the Hands-On 6.5: Search with Google link.

   The WebSim begins with an empty computer screen.

4. Use Start ⊞ →Internet Explorer to start the web browser within the WebSim.

5. Type **google.com** in the address bar and tap the ⸢Enter⸣ key.

   The Google search engine web page appears. Like many search engines, Google works best when you enter three or four words that describe what you are looking for. In this example, you will be looking for information on skiing at Mount Baker.

6. Type the word **mountain** in the Search box and tap the [Enter] key.

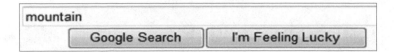

If you don't put enough information into your search, you won't end up with the information you are looking for. *Mountain* is not specific enough to get you to information about Mount Baker skiing. Notice the number of pages found at the top of the search results. (The number of results found on your computer may differ.)

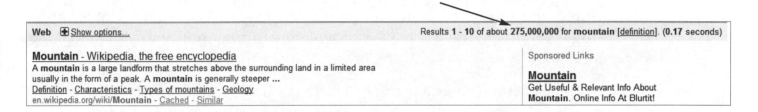

Narrow the Search

Rather than tediously going through search result pages until you see if you can find one about Mount Baker, add some keywords to narrow the search.

7. In the Search box, type **baker** and **skiing** at the end of the word *mountain* and tap the [Enter] key.

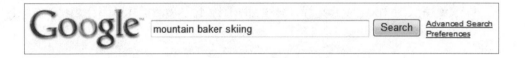

You will notice that by adding just a couple more search terms that the top hits are about the subject you are looking for. The blue text is the actual link and the title of the page, and the green text is the address of where that page is on the web.

8. Click the Mt. Baker Ski Area Winter 2009–10 link.

This will take you to the actual website where information about skiing at Mount Baker can be found.

9. Close [X] the browser window to return to the web page for this book.

You should now see the web page for this book. You will use a link on this page for the next exercise.

The World of Search Engines

In this lesson, Google is used to illustrate navigation and search concepts. Google is just one of the many *search engines* you can use to search for information on the web. The web has millions of pages stored on millions of connected computers scattered across the globe. No single search engine will always provide the information that you're looking for.

Internet Explorer has an Instant Search box to the right of the address bar.

Because of the way search engines filter the information that is shown, you can get different results from the same search words on different search engines. It is like different chefs cooking the same recipe; each has a "secret ingredient" that gives his or her results a distinct flavor.

Besides Google (www.google.com), other popular search engines include Yahoo! (www.yahoo.com), Bing from Microsoft (www.bing.com), and Ask (www.ask.com).

Many search engines also have specialized searches for specific information. Google, for example, has the ability to search just images or just news-related websites.

Google allows many types of searches, including an image search.

With all of the capabilities these search engines have to index the web, some information is still not within their reach. Many sites that generate their own content (such as newspapers, magazines, and archive sites) do not allow outside search engines to index their sites. They use search engines built into their websites that are designed specifically to search their data. To access the data from those sites, you would need to go directly to those sites. This is helpful to know if you're not finding the information you want with search engines.

Defending Yourself from Web Threats

The World Wide Web is a powerful tool giving you access to information and products. Unfortunately, it also can allow threats, such as computer viruses, access to your computer. Once your computer is connected to the Internet, you need to defend your computer against potential threats. Two types of software handle most of the defense for your computer: antivirus software and firewall software.

Firewall Software

Firewall software is one way to protect your computer from various Internet threats. The firewall acts much like the outer defensive wall on a medieval castle.

Win 7 comes with a built-in firewall. The firewall checks all data coming into the computer and blocks any data (based on rules programmed into the firewall) that is deemed a threat.

1 Your computer

2 Your firewall

3 The Internet

Antivirus Software

Computer viruses are small programs written to disrupt your computer. They can be picked up from websites, email, and various types of documents. Some viruses are irritating, others destroy files on your computer, and the worst try to steal personal information from your computer.

Antivirus software works by looking for signs (or "signatures") of viruses in all data coming into the computer and in any files being used by the computer. Some antivirus software also watches the computer for strange activity that may be a sign of a virus infection.

Updating Your Antivirus Software   Most new computers come with antivirus software installed as a free trial sample, but at some point you will need to pay for a subscription that keeps it updated. Antivirus software needs to be updated regularly because new viruses are constantly being created. Without updates, your antivirus software will slowly become less effective.

HANDS-ON 6.6 Update Virus Definitions

In this exercise, you will run a web simulation that allows you to open Norton AntiVirus and run LiveUpdate to update its virus signatures.

1. Launch Internet Explorer and enter `labpub.com/learn/silver/wtw7/` in the address bar.

   The book web page appears.

2. Click the Hands-On 6.6: Update Virus Definitions link.

   As the simulation begins, the Norton AntiVirus window is already open. In this simulation, you will run LiveUpdate manually to check for the most recent virus definitions. LiveUpdate also can run on a regular schedule automatically.

3. Click the highlighted Run LiveUpdate link under Quick Tasks near the lower-left corner of the window.

   After clicking the Run LiveUpdate link, the LiveUpdate dialog box appears.

4. Click the highlighted Start button to download and install available updates.

   LiveUpdate uses your Internet connection to check for updates to the various program components and to download available ones. (This may take a minute or so.) Then LiveUpdate installs those updates. During these processes, LiveUpdate displays their progress. When the installation is over, it displays a summary of the newly installed software.

5. Click the highlighted Close button to exit the LiveUpdate dialog box.

6. Close [X] the window to go back to the book web page.

   The web page for this book reappears. Now you can either close the Internet Explorer window or leave it open for later use.

7. Close [X] or minimize [_] the Internet Explorer window.

Using Social Media Sites Safely

Social media sites are websites where people and/or businesses with mutual interests are linked together to communicate with each other. Communications can take many forms: written posts, game play, picture and video-sharing, news-sharing, and online discussions. Visitors to a site are often encouraged to share comments or join in discussions about information posted. Social sites encourage and facilitate two-way communication.

Social media sites facilitate two-way communication in many ways.

A social media site may a have narrow or a broad focus. YouTube is a site primarily used to share videos. Two popular sites, Facebook and MySpace, are primarily social networking sites, but they also facilitate picture, video, and music sharing. Blogger provides personal and business blogs for sharing written posts but can include pictures, videos, comments, and discussions. Sites like LinkedIn specifically target businesses, while Yelp! targets people who want to share recommendations for services like restaurants.

With any Internet activity, you have to protect your privacy and be vigilant about avoiding scams and the inappropriate use of your personal information. As you link yourself with others online, keep the following information in mind:

- You should assume any information you share on the Internet may stay on the Internet *forever*. You have to be careful about what you say and be very selective with the pictures and videos you post. The information you post can resurface many years in the future, and you never know who may see it. The information could become personally embarrassing or adversely affect things like potential job opportunities.

- Never share your login and password information with anyone online. (See Passwords section of Lesson 1.)

- Always be wary of "friends" that you make online. Your trust should be given carefully to online friends. Scams can happen when online people become your friends to gather personal information. Others may take advantage of your network to spread misinformation.

Concepts Review

True/False Questions

1. A dial-up modem enables you to connect your computer to the Internet over a standard phone line.   **true** **false** _____

2. A router enables only a single computer to connect to a high-speed Internet connection.   **true** **false** _____

3. Hyperlinks are links to other pages on the web.   **true** **false** _____

4. A favorite is a web page saved in your web browser for later.   **true** **false** _____

5. Once antivirus software is installed, your computer is protected from threats—if updated regularly.   **true** **false** _____

6. The feature in Internet Explorer that lets you open multiple web pages in the same window is called tabbed browsing.   **true** **false** _____

Multiple Choice Questions

1. Which is a top-level domain?
   Page number: _____
   a. .gov
   b. .shop
   c. .buy
   d. .kid

2. Which piece of equipment is used to connect multiple computers to a high-speed Internet connection?
   Page number: _____
   a. Modem
   b. Phone line
   c. Router
   d. Network card

3. When using a search engine, it is best to enter _____.
   Page number: _____
   a. dozens of words describing what you are looking for
   b. words that vaguely describe what you're looking for to make sure you cover all potential search areas
   c. only one word that describes what you are looking for
   d. a few keywords that describe what you are looking for

4. Besides Internet Explorer, other web browsers are _____.
   Page number: _____
   a. Firefox
   b. Chrome
   c. Yahoo
   d. Both a and b

Skill Builders

SKILL BUILDER 6.1 **Create a Favorite**

In this exercise, you will create a favorite for the popular Ask search engine.

1. Start Internet Explorer using the Internet Explorer button on the taskbar.

2. Click in the address bar, type **www.ask.com**, and press the ⌷Enter⌷ key.

3. Use ⌷Ctrl⌷+⌷D⌷ from the keyboard to add a favorite.

   Keyboard shortcuts sometimes are found next to commands on drop-down menus. This shortcut to add a favorite is located on the Add to Favorites menu.

4. Make sure the Name field has a good descriptive name for the favorite. Once entered, click the Add button to continue.

   In this example, the favorite name is very descriptive. You do not need to change it.

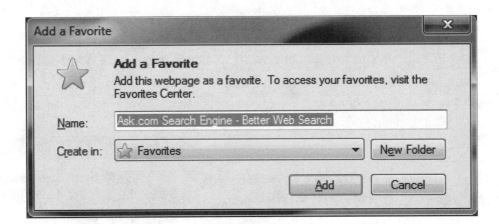

5. Press ⌷Alt⌷+⌷C⌷ on the keyboard to open the favorites list.

   Verify that your Ask.com Search Engine link is on the list.

6. Close ☒ Internet Explorer.

Search with Ask.com

 Using the Ask.com search engine, you will look for information about the Craters of the Moon National Monument.

1. Use Start→Internet Explorer to start the web browser.

2. Type **labpub.com/learn/silver/wtw7/** in the address bar and tap the Enter key.

3. Click the Skill Builder 6.2: Search with Ask.com link.
   The WebSim begins with an empty computer screen.

4. Use Start→Internet Explorer to start the web browser within the WebSim.

5. Type **ask.com** in the address bar as shown at right and tap the Enter key.
   The Ask search engine web page appears.

6. Write down two or three keywords on a piece of paper that you would use to look up information on the Craters of the Moon National Monument.

7. Type **moon** into the search box and tap the Enter key.
   Notice that Ask displays some search keyword suggestions as you type. This can be helpful, since entering just one word does not make for a good search.
   Notice the result of millions of pages found at the top of the search results.

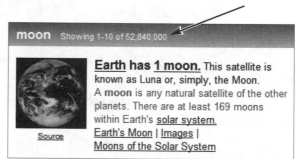

8. Click the scroll bar three times to simulate scrolling up and down to view the first page of the search results.
   Notice that none of these results contain information about the national monument. All of the web pages, images, and news stories are about the moon.

Narrow the Search

Rather than tediously go through search result pages until you see one about the national monument, let's add some keywords to narrow the search.

9. Type **crater monument** into the search box and tap the [Enter] key to run your search again.

   `moon crater monument|` 🔍

   These additional words narrow your search to thousands of hits instead of millions of hits. Did these words match what you wrote on your scratch paper?

   > Showing **1-10** of 24,300 for
   > moon crater monument

   You should see that your top three hits were exactly what you were looking for.

10. Click once with the mouse over the binoculars icon for the first link after sponsored links, shown below. (If this were the real site, you would simply point over the icon without clicking.)

    > **Craters** Of The **Moon** National **Monument** & Preserve - **Craters** Of The
    > **Craters** of the **Moon** National **Monument** and Preserve ... **Craters** of the **Moon** National **Monument** and Preserve ; P.O. Box 29 ; Arco, ID 83213 ... "a weird and scenic landscape peculiar to itself" is how President Calvin Coolidge described **Craters** of the **Moon** when he established this National **Monument** in 1924. **Craters** of the **Moon**...
    > 👓 www.nps.gov/crmo/ · Cached

    A preview of the target web page appears. Ask allows you to preview the website before actually clicking on the link. This is a special feature that few search engines have. You can see if you really want to go to that website or not.

11. Click once on the Craters of the Moon National Monument link.

    The web page for this national monument appears. This website should have all the information you would need on Craters of the Moon.

12. Close [X] the browser window.

SKILL BUILDER 6.3 Perform Your Own Live Search

In this exercise, you will perform a search using Google along with your own keywords. Because you are using your own keywords, your search results may not look the same as the examples shown.

You will be searching for information on the USS Arizona Memorial, which is located in Pearl Harbor, Hawaii. You want information specifically about the memorial, not Pearl Harbor.

If you find the site www.nps.gov/usar listed in the top four or five listings in your search returns, then you have accomplished a successful search.

1. Start Internet Explorer with Start→Internet.

2. Click in the address bar, type **google.com**, and press the ‹Enter› key.

3. On a piece a paper, jot down four words or names (which may contain more than one word) that you think would help you find the information you are looking for.

For most searches, you shouldn't need more than four words—if you have the correct four.

4. Click in the Google search box, type in the two best words you have on your list, and press the ‹Enter› key.

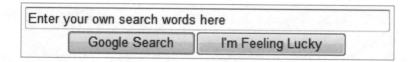

Did you find the target website with your search words? Was it anywhere on the page?

5. Go back into the Google search box, type in one more additional search word from your list, and press ‹Enter›.

Did you find the target website? Was it farther up the search list?

6. If you found the target website, go ahead and close ▣ X ▣ your browser and end the exercise. If you had problems, continue searching.

Find One Solution

Remember, there are many ways to search for an answer using a search engine. Here are four words/names you might have used, in order of importance: USS Arizona, Pearl Harbor, Memorial, Hawaii.

7. In the Google search box, type **uss arizona** and tap the ⌈Enter⌉ key.

Web	Results **1 - 10** of about **1,020,000** for **USS Arizona**

USS Arizona National Memorial (U.S. National Park Service)
Official National Park Service site for the memorial that straddles the sunken hull of
the battleship **USS Arizona** and commemorates the December 7, 1941, ...
www.nps.gov/usar/ - 34k - Cached - Similar pages - Note this

This search string is perfect: The target site is the first hit in the search.

8. Close ⊠ the Internet Explorer window.

Using the Control Panel and Help

Your Win 7 computer came with a certain look and features set to work certain ways. What if you want to change Win 7? Decide to change the way it looks? Want to change the way things are done? Don't like the background on the Desktop and want to add your favorite picture? Opt to uninstall a program you never use? You can make those changes using Win 7's Control Panel.

Windows Help and Support makes the process easy. It can teach you what you can do, tell you how to do it, and jump you to the correct Control Panel location. With the Control Panel and Help and Support, you can maintain your computer, uninstall or repair programs, change the resolution on your screen, update security features, and do much more. They put *you* in control of Win 7.

LESSON OBJECTIVES

After studying this lesson, you will be able to:

- Search Windows Help and Support
- Install and uninstall programs
- Change the screen resolution and the background
- Run Disk Defragmenter
- Create a restore point and use System Restore

Additional learning resources are available at **labpub.com/learn/silver/wtw7/**

Case Study: Installing and Uninstalling Programs

Brendan has gotten a new version of Adobe Photoshop Elements® for his notebook computer to edit pictures from his digital camera. He gets a friend to help him install it, and it is easier than he expected. They put the program disc in the DVD drive, and an AutoPlay box pops up. From there, it is just a matter of following the onscreen prompts.

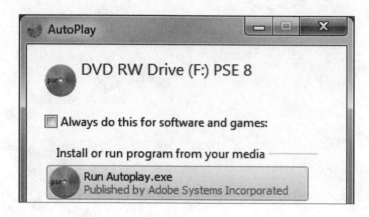

When you install a program from a disc, Win 7 usually will provide an AutoPlay box to help you get started.

A few days after installing the new version, Brendan decides to uninstall the older version of Photoshop Elements. In the Control Panel, Brendan finds an Uninstall a Program link that takes him to the proper window. He sees that Adobe Photoshop Elements 6.0 is near the top of the alphabetical list. When he gives the command to uninstall the program, Win 7 walks him through the process with ease. Brendan now has extra storage space for his digital pictures.

Features in the Control Panel Home view are grouped into categories.

Using Windows Help and Support

Windows Help and Support is built into Win 7, and it is a great place to start when you have a question concerning Win 7. You can search for answers two ways: by typing in search words or by clicking through contents choices. Help and Support will not only provide information and instructions about your topic, but it also will often provide quick links to the program or feature needed to carry out the instructions. Help and Support has information that is specific to Win 7. To get help with other programs, you must open Help within each program.

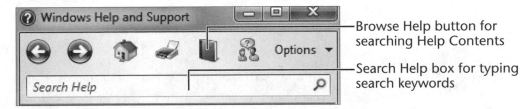

Browse Help button for searching Help Contents

Search Help box for typing search keywords

Help and Support lets you search two ways: contents or keywords.

Searching by Contents

Browse Help is much like searching the table of contents in a book. A contents list of Help topics and categories is displayed. A Help topic is linked to articles with information and instructions about the topic. Help categories (like a folder) can contain Help topics or other categories. As you navigate through the lists, you gain understanding about other aspects of the topic, and you can also discover useful keywords.

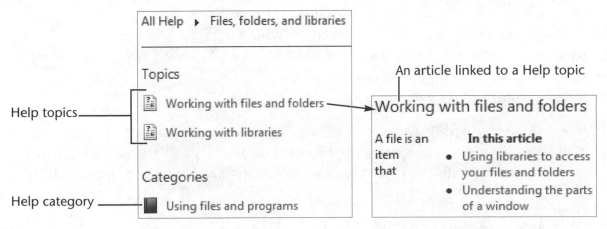

Help topics

Help category

An article linked to a Help topic

Browse Help lets you search Contents like a table of contents.

Searching by Keyword

Using the Search box in Help and Support is like using the index of a book. A keyword or two can be typed into the box to search for information or instructions related to the search words. Instead of Help categories and Help topics, a keyword search will generate a numbered list of results linked to articles related to the keywords.

1. Create a new folder
2. Configure Bluetooth sharing
3. Create or delete a shortcut

A keyword search in Help and Support produces a numbered list of results.

 TIP! A Contents search can be time-consuming. If you think you have good keywords, try a keyword search first. If that doesn't work, try a Contents search.

 HANDS-ON 7.1 **Search for Information in Help and Support**

In this exercise, you will use a Contents search and a keyword search in Help and Support to find information about creating a new folder.

1. Choose Start ⊞→Help and Support (in the right pane) to open Windows Help and Support.

Most computer manufacturers place their logo on the Help and Support home page along with links to their websites for support, registration, and more.

Do a Contents Search

2. Click the Browse Help button on the toolbar to search Contents, as shown at right.

Review the first Contents list to determine the category most related to creating a new folder.

3. Click once to display Files, Folders, and Libraries in the Contents list.

There are several new Help categories ▋ and a few Help topics ▤ near the top of the list. One is a Help category related to creating: Creating, Opening and Saving. Which would you click next?

4. Click the Creating, Opening and Saving Help category.

Notice that there are no Help categories ▋, just Help topics ▤.

5. Choose the Help topic Create a New Folder.

6. Briefly review the article.

Keyword Search

Now you will use a different method to locate a Help topic.

7. Click in the Search box, type **create folders**, and tap Enter .

Notice that there are no Help categories or topics. Help and Support displays a numbered list of results that relate to the words *folders* or *create*.

8. From the list choose Create a New Folder.

The keyword search has quickly jumped you to the Create a New Folder article you reviewed in step 5.

9. Close ▄▄ X ▄▄ Help and Support.

Using the Control Panel

The Control Panel is a very important area in Win 7. It provides access to most of the programs and features necessary to change the screen appearance and the way things work in Win 7.

Control Panel Views

The Control Panel can be displayed in one of three views: Category, Large Icons, or Small Icons. The Control Panel view changes if a different command is chosen in the View By drop-down menu.

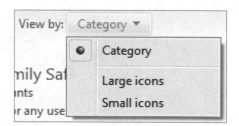

Category View   In the Category view, tasks are grouped into eight categories: System and Security; Network and Internet; Hardware and Sound; Programs; User Accounts and Family Safety; Appearance and Personalization;

Clock, Language, and Region; and Ease of Access. As a new user, you may find this view easier to use than the others because you do not need to know the names of the features (programs) that are used for the different tasks.

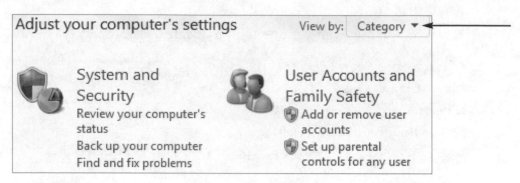

Win 7 was designed to be highly personalized for each user, and Control Panel is the place to set your personalization options. Shown here are two of the eight categories in the Category view.

You can access settings two ways in Category view: You can click an item in one of the eight categories or use a keyword search (similar to Contents and keyword searches in Help and Support). You also can find links to the Control Panel through Help and Support.

Large Icons and Small Icons Views   In the Large Icons and Small Icons views, tasks are accessed with file icons. These classic views have been available in past versions of Windows and are often favored by longtime users familiar with the filenames.

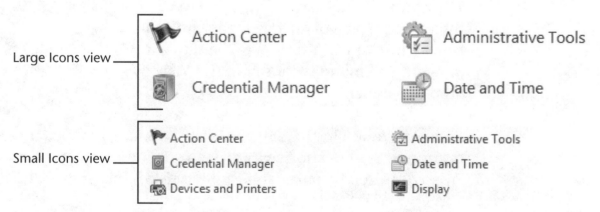

Large Icons and Small Icons display file icons. Control Panel views are easily changed in the View By menu.

HANDS-ON 7.2 Change the Time and Date in the Control Panel

In this exercise, you will change the date and time using a category search and a word search in the Control Panel.

If your computer lab does not allow students to access the Control Panel, you should use the WebSim for this exercise instead. Before starting with step 1, follow these steps to display the WebSim:

- Open your web browser, enter **labpub.com/learn/silver/wtw7/** in the address bar, and tap Enter .
- Click the Hands-On 7.2: Change Time and Date in the Control Panel link.
- Tap the F11 key to maximize the window if necessary.

Now you can follow the instructions in this exercise to change the date and time via the simulation. If a step for the simulation differs at all from these instructions, an onscreen note will appear.

Navigate Control Panel Categories

The Home view of the Control Panel organizes all controls into categories. This may make it easier to find some controls.

1. Open the Control Panel with Start ⊕→Control Panel.

2. Choose View By→Category, if necessary.
   The 8 categories are displayed.

3. Locate and click the Clock, Language, and Region category label.

4. Choose Set the Time and Date in the Date and Time category.

5. In the Date and Time dialog box, click the Change Date and Time button.

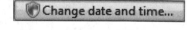

6. If you are asked provide an administrative password, type it and click OK.

   You may need an administrative password to complete steps 7 and 8. If you do not have a password, click the Cancel button and skip to step 9.

7. Follow these steps to change the date and time:

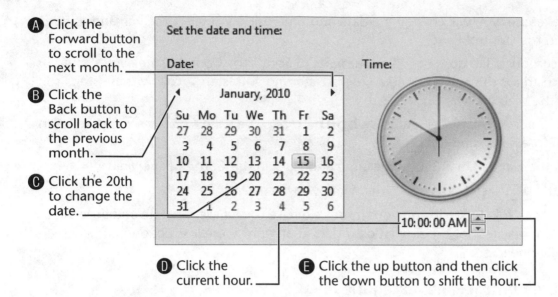

Ⓐ Click the Forward button to scroll to the next month.

Ⓑ Click the Back button to scroll back to the previous month.

Ⓒ Click the 20th to change the date.

Set the date and time:

Date:

◄ January, 2010 ►

Su	Mo	Tu	We	Th	Fr	Sa
27	28	29	30	31	1	2
3	4	5	6	7	8	9
10	11	12	13	14	15	16
17	18	19	20	21	22	23
24	25	26	27	28	29	30
31	1	2	3	4	5	6

Time:

10: 00: 00 AM

Ⓓ Click the current hour.

Ⓔ Click the up button and then click the down button to shift the hour.

In this situation, there is no need to actually change the date and time, so you will leave the dialog box without making any changes.

8. Click the Cancel button.

9. Close [X] the Date and Time dialog box.

Search with a Keyword

You can also search for a control via the Search Box on the Control Panel.

10. Choose Control Panel Home at the top of the left pane.

11. Click in the Search box and type **date**.

You jump to the same category (Date and Time) with the same link (Set the Time and Date) that was reached with category search above. Sometimes you will find a word search easier to use than a category search.

12. Close [X] the browser window for the WebSim but not the one for the book web page.

You will run another WebSim in the next exercise.

Installing and Uninstalling Software

From time to time, you may want to add a new program onto your computer. Programs you buy at the store usually come on CDs or DVDs, but many programs can be downloaded from the Internet. Either way, they need to be properly installed on your computer. If you want to remove (uninstall) a program, there is a proper way to do that as well. Now you will learn the different ways these tasks are handled by Win 7.

What Happens During Installation

When you install programs, Win 7 moves copies of the program files into folders on the C: drive. The files are put in more than one location. Most of the program files are stored in a subfolder in the Program Files folder. Some of the files are moved into the Windows folder. Win 7 also will add commands to access the program in the Start menu and possibly on the Desktop or Notification Area.

Installing Software from a Disc

Programs you install from a CD or DVD usually are designed to use Win 7's AutoPlay feature (similar to your USB flash drive). AutoPlay will automatically display a dialog box to help you get started. AutoPlay might give you the choice to run (install), uninstall, change, or repair the program.

A program CD or DVD usually will display an AutoPlay box with a run (install) choice.

QUICK REFERENCE: Installing a Program from the AutoPlay Dialog Box

Task	Procedure
Install a program from a CD or DVD	• Load the CD or DVD by opening the drive drawer, carefully placing the disc in the tray (or snapping it to the hub if necessary), and closing the drawer.
	• Wait a moment for Win 7 to display an AutoPlay dialog box. Click the command to run whichever installation program Win 7 identifies on the disc.
	• Follow the step-by-step instructions provided by the InstallShield Wizard or similar installation utility started from the disc.

 NOTE! Because students are not allowed to install software on classroom computers, the following exercise will run from a WebSim. The simulation will match what you would see if you had the actual installation CD in your computer.

 HANDS-ON 7.3 Install a Program from a Disc

 In this exercise, you will run a WebSim that simulates installing new software from a program CD. In this example, it's Adobe's popular Photoshop Elements image editing program.

Before You Begin: The book's web page should be open in Internet Explorer.

1. Click the Hands-On 7.3: Install a Program from a Disc link.

   The WebSim loads, showing you an open CD drive with the program disc.

2. Click the disc to simulate loading the software disc into the drive.

   An AutoPlay window appears.

3. From the AutoPlay window, choose Run Setup.exe.

   Your screen may look slightly different from the figure shown here.

   > Install or run program from your media
   >
   > Run Autoplay.exe
   > Published by Adobe Systems Incorpora

 NOTE! When installing the program at home, you may have to give administrative permission at this point.

4. Choose Install Adobe Photoshop Elements 8.

Install Adobe® Photoshop® Elements 8

5. Adobe asks for a language choice; you can click the drop-down menu and choose your language. Since we're using English, choose OK.

   Windows Installer prepares to install. This process takes a few moments, and the InstallShield Wizard appears.

6. Read each window as you go through the wizard.

   Adobe's End-User License Agreement (EULA) displays. To install the program, you must accept the EULA to continue. You can scroll through the agreement and read the terms.

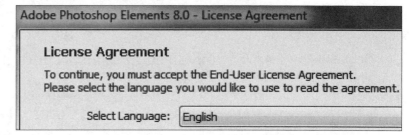

7. Click Accept if you agree with terms of the EULA. (The installation will end if you decline.)

8. Choose the country from the drop-down list and click Next. Do *not* type the serial number in the simulation.

   The serial number usually is found on the outside of the disc package.

9. To accept the default destination folder, choose Next.

   The program is copied into the Program Files folder. Advanced users could have chosen another location from here.

10. When you are asked to begin the installation, choose Install.

    The InstallShield begins to copy files onto the hard drive. This can take several minutes.

    When files are installed, many programs will ask you to restart your computer before the program can be used. This program does not require restarting.

11. Choose Finish.

    Notice that Adobe has added a program shortcut on your Desktop and a command in the Start menu.

12. Close [X] the Internet Explorer window for the WebSim but not the one for the book web page.

Uninstalling or Changing a Program

When you want to uninstall a program, it is important that you use the Uninstall feature in Win 7 to make sure all the bits and pieces of the program are removed. There are several reasons for uninstalling a program:

- It may be a program you never use, and you want to free up storage space.

- You may want to replace it with a different program.

- You may need to uninstall and then reinstall to correct a problem.

You access the Uninstall feature from the Programs category in the Control Panel.

The Control Panel provides an easy way to uninstall programs you no longer need.

The Uninstall or Change a Program window displays a long list of programs installed on your computer. In addition to removing programs, you may be able to use features in this window to make changes to or to repair a program. Each program determines whether Uninstall, Change, or Repair will be available on the window toolbar.

Task	Purpose
Uninstall	Removes the program and all related pieces such as shortcuts
Change	The program remains, but features are added or deleted from the program
Repair	The program remains, but an attempt is made to correct any damage
Uninstall and reinstall	Removes the problem program, and then a new copy of the program is installed on the computer

HANDS-ON 7.4 Uninstall a Program

In this exercise, you will run a WebSim that simulates uninstalling a program.

Before You Begin: The book's web page should be open in Internet Explorer.

1. Click the Hands-On 7.4: Uninstall a Program link.

   The WebSim loads, showing a blank Desktop.

2. Open the Control Panel by choosing Start ⊕→Control Panel.

3. Choose Uninstall a Program from the Programs category.

4. Click once to select Adobe Photoshop Elements 8.0 from the program list.

5. Choose the Uninstall button on the window toolbar.

6. Choose Next to start the InstallShield Wizard.

7. Choose Next to remove the program.

   You are warned that the program will be removed and will no longer be available.

8. Choose Remove.

   The InstallShield Wizard uninstalls the program and its related files and folders. This can take a few minutes.

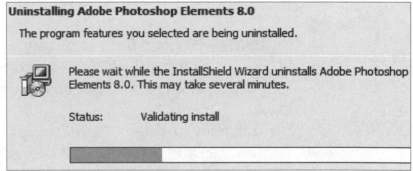

9. Choose Finish.

10. Close ▇X▇ the Control Panel window.

11. Close ▇X▇ the browser window.

Downloading Programs from the Web

Instead of buying a program on a CD or DVD, it is now common to download programs from the web—that is, to transfer a copy of the program from the web onto your computer. It is important that you verify that the program is compatible with your version of Windows (Win 7) before you start the download.

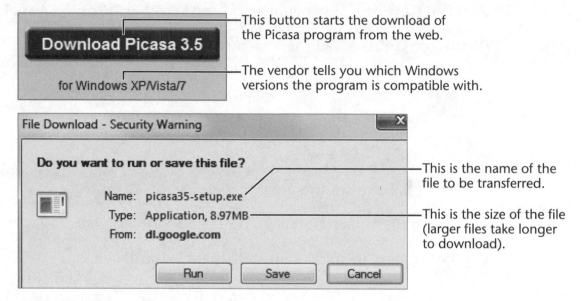

This button starts the download of the Picasa program from the web.

The vendor tells you which Windows versions the program is compatible with.

This is the name of the file to be transferred.

This is the size of the file (larger files take longer to download).

Picasa is a photo organizer program that can be downloaded from the web.

NOTE! Program files can be very large, and it can take a long time to transfer the files to your computer (the length of time is substantially longer with a dial-up connection).

Install Now or Later   *Downloading* (transferring files from the web to your computer) and *installing* (incorporating the files into your computer system) are two separate steps in the process of using downloaded programs. In the File Download box (see the preceding illustration) you are given two choices:

• **Run:** Have the program file both transfer and install now. You may need administrative permission to install a program.

• **Save:** Transfer the file now but install the program later (again, if you have the administrative permissions to install programs).

Task	Procedure
Download a program from the web to install later	• Navigate to the web page from which the program can be downloaded. • Click the download link or button. (This can vary from one website to another.) • Choose Save when Internet Explorer asks what you wish to do with the download. You also should choose a storage location on your computer, such as the Downloads folder for your login name. 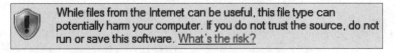 • Choose Open Folder when the download is completed. • Double-click to start the installation program, or wait to install it until later. You may need administrative permission to install a program.

Security Concerns   When you download a program, the File Download box probably will show a security warning similar to the following figure.

While files from the Internet can be useful, this file type can potentially harm your computer. If you do not trust the source, do not run or save this software. What's the risk?

A typical security warning displayed when downloading a program

Downloading anything from the web carries some risk. Files, pictures, emails, advertisements, or games can hide viruses or other malicious programs. If you have installed security software such as that discussed in Lesson 6, Using the Internet, you will greatly reduce your chances of having a security problem.

Controlling the Screen

One of the many customizations you can make in Win 7 is to change the resolution of your monitor. Resolution changes the visual appearance of the images on the screen, making objects more or less crisp, or larger or smaller.

Screen Resolution Settings

The digital images you see on your monitor are made up of tiny colored squares called pixels (picture elements). The resolution setting of a monitor establishes how many pixels are displayed horizontally and vertically. A screen setting of 800 × 600 pixels is considered low resolution. The pixels are large and may make images have jagged edges. A higher resolution setting like 1,280 × 800 displays more pixels in the same space, so the pixels are smaller. Some other results of choosing a higher resolution:

- Smaller pixels can display finer lines, so images and text look sharper.

- Smaller pixels create smaller images and text, allowing more images and text to fit on the screen.

- Smaller text will be sharper but may be harder to read.

Using the Control Panel, you can change screen resolution on most monitors from as low as 800 × 600 to 1,600 × 1,280 or higher.

When it is magnified several hundred percent, you can see that the Recycle Bin icon is made up of square pixels of different shades and colors.

LCD Monitors and Aspect Ratios

To take advantage of Win 7's marvelous graphics capabilities, people are more often than not opting to buy flat-panel LCD (liquid crystal display) monitors with their new computers. Because of their trim size and lighter weight, they take up less room on your desktop and are easier to set up and move around than older-style monitors. They also are available in a variety of sizes and shapes.

LCD Panels and Wide Screens

Older-style CRT (cathode ray tube) monitors had one screen shape but different diagonal measurements—14-inch, 15-inch, 17-inch, 19-inch, 20-inch, and so on. Newer LCD panels vary in both size and shape. The viewable screen is measured diagonally to determine LCD size (CRT sizing often includes the case).

Different Resolutions; Different Aspect Ratios LCD screens are assembled with a fixed number of liquid crystals horizontally and vertically (referred to as their native resolution). Although screens have a native resolution, the resolution or number of pixels displayed horizontally and vertically can be changed (see the Changing Monitor Resolution Quick Reference table on page 220). Changing the resolution also may change the *aspect ratio* of

With some resolution settings, monitors may display in letterbox (with black bands).

the screen. If you change to a resolution setting with fewer pixels than the native resolution, the unused screen pixels may appear as black bands above and below (letterbox).

Behind the Screen *(continued)*

Standard and Widescreen Aspect Ratios CRT screens (older computer monitors and non-HD TVs) have an aspect ratio of 4:3 (for every four pixels displayed horizontally, three pixels are displayed vertically).

Common aspect ratios for LCD panels

LCD screens are available in several aspect ratios, including 4:3. LCD screens with aspect ratios of 15:9, 16:9, or 16:10 would be called *widescreen*. When you adjust screen resolution in the Control Panel, you also may be changing the displayed aspect ratio.

QUICK REFERENCE: Changing Monitor Resolution

Task	Procedure
Locate the Display Setting dialog box	• Open the Control Panel with Start ⊕→Control Panel.
	• From the category Appearance and Personalization, choose Adjust Screen Resolution.
	• The Display Settings dialog box appears and displays a slider to adjust resolution with the current resolution (number of pixels horizontally and vertically) shown below the slider.
Change the resolution	• Move the slider to another position.
	• Click Apply.
	• The screen may go dark momentarily and then return with the new resolution. (If the resolution is higher, items on the screen look smaller. If the settings are lower, the items look larger.)
	• Click Yes before 15 seconds, or the resolution will revert back to its original settings.
	• If you get a warning saying "Resolution setting not supported," do *not* click any buttons. Let the program revert back to the original resolution and then try a different resolution.
	• Click Yes in the prompt box to accept the resolution settings.

Changing the Background Image

The background (also called the wallpaper) of the Desktop can be personalized to show a solid color or your favorite image. Computer manufacturers often place their logos on the background or make you stare at a design or color that is unpleasant. It is easy and fun to change the background color or image. You can have a picture of friends, relatives, pets, or favorite places. If you own a digital camera, you have an endless supply of possible images.

TIP! Avoid images with clutter or colors that make it difficult to see your Desktop icons.

QUICK REFERENCE: Changing the Desktop Background

Task	Procedure
Locate the Desktop Background window	• Open the Control Panel by choosing Start→Control Panel. • From the category Appearance and Personalization, choose Change Desktop Background.
Change the background of the Desktop	• Drop down the Picture Location menu and choose Solid Colors or the Picture Library for your pictures from the list. • From the viewing area, click a color or a picture to add to the background (you may have to scroll). Your selection will be displayed on the Desktop. You can minimize all windows to see the background more clearly. • If you have selected a picture, you are asked how to position the picture. Choose the control for Fill, Fit, Stretch, Tile, or Center. • Click OK.

NOTE! Try This at Home 7.1 at the end of this lesson gives guided practice in changing your Desktop background.

Defragmenting Drives

Your computer's hard drive and removable drives (such as USB flash drives) can become fragmented and cluttered as you use your computer. Files are saved, edited, or deleted and can become scattered (fragmented) on your hard drive. Fragmentation occurs because Win 7 assigns an empty space on the disk the first time you save a file, but each time you make changes to the file, those changes will be saved in empty spaces elsewhere. Win 7 knows that the pieces are tied together, but too much fragmentation makes Win 7 work harder and slowly. Clutter comes from pieces left behind when a program is uninstalled or temporary files that are no longer needed are not removed. Win 7 provides features to fix these problems.

Defragmentation

There is a program in the Control Panel to fix fragmentation. Disk Defragmenter reunites the related bits and pieces and fills the gaps left when programs were uninstalled or files were deleted.

Scheduling Defragmentation   The defragmentation (also called "defrag") process can sometimes take an hour or more. It makes sense to run the process when you do not need to use the computer. The Disk Defragmenter program has a Modify Schedule feature that lets you schedule the process to run automatically when it least affects you. Though you can choose daily or weekly, most new users will find that the monthly option is adequate.

 HANDS-ON 7.5   Use the Disk Defragmenter

 In this exercise, you will locate Disk Defragmenter in the Control Panel.

Before You Begin: This book's web page should be open in Internet Explorer.

1. Click the Hands-On 7.5: Using the Disk Defragmenter link.

   The WebSim loads, showing a blank Desktop.

2. Open the Control Panel with Start ⊞→Control Panel.

3. Type **defrag** in the Search box at the top-right corner of the Control Panel window and tap ⌷Enter⌷.

   The Control Panel filtered its choices as you typed. It now displays the command Defragment Your Hard Drive.

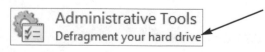

4. Click the Defragment Your Hard Drive link.

   The dialog box that appears enables you to schedule automatic defragmentation (recommended). The Defragment Now button runs a manual defrag.

5. Click the Defragment Disk button.

   The defragmenting process begins. The time to defrag varies widely but can take an hour or more. So you will cancel the command for now.

Progress
Pass 9: 72% consolidated

6. Click the Stop Operation button.

   The Defragment Now command is best run at the end of the day when you are done using the computer. However, you can pause or cancel the command whenever necessary.

7. Close ❎ all windows and close the browser window.

Using Windows Update

Win 7 is a very complex operating system with many components. From time to time, protection against security threats, corrections to errors in the programming, or new features and improvements

Windows Update
Check for updates
Turn automatic updating

will be made available as updates. You can periodically go online, download the updates, and then install them on your computer. An easier way to keep your system updated is to have this done automatically using Windows Update.

During the update process, other Microsoft product updates may be included, such as Internet Explorer or Microsoft Office programs.

What Windows Update Does

There are three main kinds of updates:

- **Important:** These updates deal with security and reliability problems.

- **Recommended:** These updates focus on less critical issues or enhancements to Win 7.

- **Optional:** These updates, such as new games or other nonessential files, are considered optional updates.

The Update Process   Windows Update starts the process by going online to Microsoft's update site, and then the process takes place in steps:

- **Compare:** Win 7 compares a list of available updates on the web with updates already installed on your computer.

- **Recommendations:** Win 7 recommends a list of updates for your version of Win 7 that have not yet been installed. You can accept or reject updates.

- **Download:** Copies of the update files are downloaded (transferred) from the web to your computer.

- **Install:** The downloaded files must be installed to replace existing files or add new files.

- **Restart:** Often, your computer needs to be restarted to put the new changes into effect.

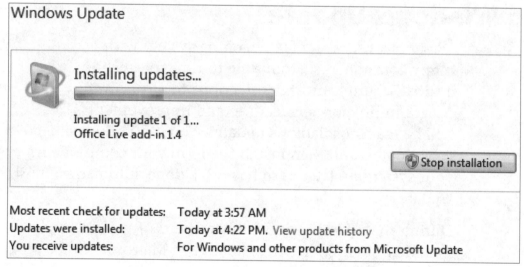

Windows Update displays the progress of checking for updates.

Automatic vs. Manual Updating

You can choose to check for and download updates automatically, or you can choose to do those manually. (Optional files are not downloaded automatically.)

Two advantages of automatic updating are:

- You will not have to remember to check for updates on a regular basis.

- Checking for updates and initiating downloads will happen in the background while you do other tasks.

Installation of downloaded updates is a separate task. You can choose to make the installation step automatic or manual as well.

NOTE! Skill Builder 7.2 gives you an opportunity to practice scheduling when Windows Update checks for new updates.

QUICK REFERENCE: Running Windows Update

Task	Procedure
Set Windows Update to check for updates automatically	• Choose Start ⊞→Control Panel. • In the Search box type **windows**. • From the Windows Update category, choose Turn Automatic Updating On or Off. • Choose the control for Install Updates Automatically (recommended). You can also change the day and time to install the updates. • Choose OK. • Type your password if asked and choose OK. • Close ▮ X ▮ the Control Panel window.
Run Windows Update yourself	• Choose Start ⊞→All Programs→Windows Update. • Click the Check for Updates button and wait a few moments while Win 7 checks on the web for any new updates. • Choose View Available Updates. • From the list of updates that appears, select the control boxes for the updates that you want to install. • Click the Install button. • Type your password if asked and choose OK. Wait while Win 7 downloads and installs the update files. • When told the updates were successfully installed, ▮ X ▮ close the Control Panel window.

What Happens During the Installation Process?

When update files are downloaded, copies of the files are transferred to your computer. Those files then need to be installed. During the installation process, files that have errors or have become obsolete are moved (to be available later should you need to uninstall or perform a System Restore) and replaced with the updated versions. Files for new features are added to the appropriate folders. Often, you will be asked to restart your computer after the installation is complete. The startup process will launch the new versions and enable them to take effect.

The Trend Toward Automatic Updates

Automatic updates have become a common software feature as software has gotten more complicated. At the same time, more people have access to the Internet (especially high-speed Internet), which makes it easier for developers to send updates electronically.

Before the web, people rarely got updates for their software. They often had to live with any flaws or problems in the software until the next version was available for sale. On occasion, when a flaw was bad enough to make the software unusable, a company might mail registered users a floppy disk with corrections or a corrected version of the program. This happened rarely because it was very expensive for the companies. The web has changed that.

Companies now can post updates on their websites or, better yet, provide automatic updating built into their programs. When automatic updating detects an Internet connection, a program can "call home" and check for updates that add new or improved features or patches to fix problems. These update files are then automatically transferred to your computer. They either will be automatically installed or you will be prompted to install them.

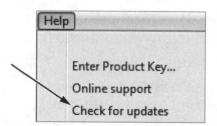

In many programs that do not have automatic updates, you can manually check for updates. This is generally done by looking for the update command on the Help menu.

Although automatic updates can be convenient, they also can be annoying when they interrupt too often while you are trying to work. Programs with automatic update procedures may enable you to set how frequently and at what time of the day they look for updates. You also may have choices about how automatic or manual the process will be.

Using System Restore

System Restore is a Win 7 program that can save certain settings on your computer (called a restore point) and then, if necessary in the future, restore Win 7 back to its state on that date. Restore points can be created automatically, or you can manually create a restore point whenever you think it necessary.

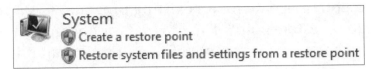
System
Create a restore point
Restore system files and settings from a restore point

The Control Panel gives access to System Restore.

How It Works

System Restore resets the system back to its state at the time the restore point was created. A restore point saves information about the *registry*, the place where Win 7 settings are stored. It also stores information about the files responsible for starting system programs and application programs such as games, email, word processing, and so on.

If a program gets installed but does not seem to work correctly or causes other things to work strangely, you can do a System Restore. System Restore will let you choose a date and time earlier than the installation and reset Win 7 back to its state on that day and time. The newly installed program is deleted, and Win 7's settings are returned to what they were on the prior date.

System Restore can help fix problems that might be making your computer run slowly or stop responding.

System Restore does not affect any of your documents, pictures, or other personal data. Recently installed programs and drivers might be uninstalled. Is this process reversible?

System Restore resets Win 7 files from an earlier time without affecting your data files.

**WARNING!** A restore point saves information about Win 7 programming but *does not* save information about your personal files. You should make regular backups (copies) of *your* files onto CDs, DVDs, or an external hard drive.

Automatic Restore Points

Win 7 will usually create restore points automatically every day (if your computer is turned on) and before most programs or files are installed. If you want to be certain that there is a current restore point, you also can choose to create a restore point manually at any time.

When to Manually Make a Restore Point If you are going to install a new program or accept an update for an existing program, it is a good idea to manually create a restore point. The program or update may also automatically create a restore point before it installs, but it is better to be safe than sorry. If something does not work right after the installation is complete, you will be able to do a System Restore back to the point just before the install. Hopefully, the newly created problem will be fixed.

!NOTE! Skill Builder 7.1 gives you an opportunity to practice manually creating a restore point.

QUICK REFERENCE: Manually Creating a Restore Point

Task	Procedure
Locate the System Properties box	• Choose Start →Control Panel. • Type **restore point** in the Search box. • From the System category, choose Create a Restore Point. • At this point you may be asked for an administrative password. If asked, type in the password and click OK.
Create a manual restore point	• From the System Protection tab, click on the Create button. • You can type a description to identify the reason for the restore point. Type **Restore point test** (Win 7 will add the date and time automatically). • Click the Create button. • It takes a few moments while the restore point is created. When the process is finished, you will be told it was created successfully. Click the OK button.

Concepts Review

True/False Questions

1. If you know what you are searching for, a keyword search is usually faster than a Contents search. **true** **false** _____

2. A system restore can restore damaged documents or pictures. **true** **false** _____

3. A keyword search in Windows Help and Support is similar to using the index of a book. **true** **false** _____

4. A program downloaded from the web could potentially contain a computer virus. **true** **false** _____

5. Increasing the resolution setting for the monitor makes small text sharper but also smaller. **true** **false** _____

6. Win 7 can automatically run Windows Update for you. **true** **false** _____

Multiple Choice Questions

1. Access to settings that let you personalize your computer can be found in _____.
   Page number: _____
   a. Help and Support
   b. The Control Panel
   c. The menu when you right-click on the Desktop background
   d. All of the above

2. Which of the following is a reason you might uninstall a program?
   Page number: _____
   a. You want to free up storage space.
   b. You want to replace it with a different program.
   c. You are trying to correct a problem with the program.
   d. All of the above

3. Downloading a program means _____.
   Page number: _____
   a. transferring program files to the web
   b. installing program files on your computer
   c. transferring program files from the web
   d. uninstalling program files on your computer

4. Windows Updates can be _____.
   Page number: _____
   a. downloaded manually
   b. installed manually
   c. downloaded and installed automatically
   d. All of the above

Skill Builders

Create a Restore Point

In this exercise, you will create a restore point. You will need administrative permission to create a restore point.

On the Web

If your computer lab does not allow students to access the Control Panel, you should use the WebSim for this exercise instead. Before starting with step 1, follow these steps to display the WebSim:

- Open your web browser, enter **labpub.com/learn/silver/wtw7/** in the address bar, and tap Enter.
- Click the Skill Builder 7.1: Create a Restore Point link.
- Tap the F11 key to maximize the window if necessary.

Now you can follow the instructions in this exercise to create a restore point via the simulation. If a step for the simulation differs at all from these instructions, an onscreen note will appear.

1. Open the Control Panel with Start→Control Panel.

2. Type **restore point** in the Search box.

3. From the System category, click Create a Restore Point. If you are asked for an administrative password, type in the password.

   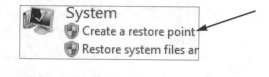

   The System Properties box appears, and the System Protection tab should be selected.

   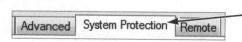

4. From the Available Drives list, make sure the protection for Local Disk (C:) is set to On.

   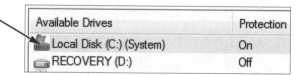

5. Click the Create button.

   You are asked to type a description that will help you identify the purpose of the restore point. Win 7 will add the date and time for you.

6. Type **Sample: before installing Program X**.

7. Click the Create button.

   Win 7 creates a restore point (this takes a few moments) and then advises you, "The restore point was created successfully."

8. Click Close.

9. Close  the browser window for the WebSim but not the one for the book web page.

Schedule Windows Updates

In this exercise, you will schedule the frequency and time for Windows Updates. You will need administrative permission to complete all steps.

If your computer lab does not allow students to access the Control Panel, you should use the WebSim for this exercise instead. If this book's web page is not already open, open your web browser, enter **labpub.com/learn/silver/wtw7/** in the address bar, and tap Enter.

1. Click the Skill Builder 7.2: Schedule Windows Update link. If a step for the simulation differs at all from these instructions, an onscreen note will appear.

2. Tap F11 to maximize the window if necessary.

3. Open the Control Panel with Start→Control Panel.

4. In the search box, type **windows**.

5. From the Windows Update category, click Turn Automatic Updating On or Off.

> Windows Update
> Check for updates
> Turn automatic updating on or off

6. Follow these steps to schedule automatic updates and installations:

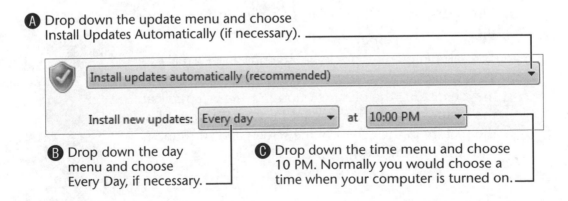

Ⓐ Drop down the update menu and choose Install Updates Automatically (if necessary).

Ⓑ Drop down the day menu and choose Every Day, if necessary.

Ⓒ Drop down the time menu and choose 10 PM. Normally you would choose a time when your computer is turned on.

7. Click OK.

8. If asked for administrative permission, click Close.

9. Close  all windows.

 **Try This at Home**

TRY THIS AT HOME 7.1 **Change the Screen Background**

In this exercise, you will add an image to your Desktop background.

1. Open the Control Panel by choosing Start→Control Panel.

2. In the Appearance and Personalization category, click Change Desktop Background.

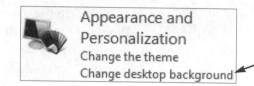

3. Click the Picture Location menu ▼ button and choose Picture Library.

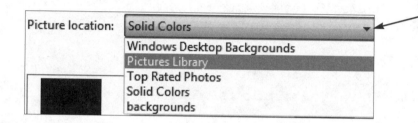

4. Click to select one of the pictures you would like on your Desktop background.

As pictures are selected, they replace the background. Windows can be moved or minimized so you can see the background more clearly.

5. Drop down the Picture Position menu and choose Fit.

The sample pictures are large, so choosing Fit makes sense. If you choose a small picture, Fit will stretch (and maybe distort) the picture. Choosing Tile will duplicate the picture like tiles on a wall. Choosing Center will place the picture in the center of the screen and surround it with the most recently chosen solid color.

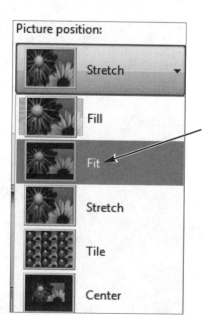

6. Click Save Changes.

7. Close [X] all windows.

Change Your Screen Resolution

In this exercise, you will change the resolution of the monitor on your home computer system.

1. Open the Control Panel with Start→Control Panel.

2. In the Appearance and Personalization category, choose Adjust Screen Resolution.

3. Choose the Resolution drop-down menu.

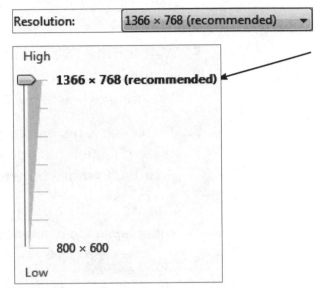

The Display Setting dialog box appears. There should be a slider to adjust resolution with the current resolution displayed beside the slider.

!NOTE! The resolution settings indicated by your computer may differ from the settings shown in the exercise figures.

4. Write down the current resolution setting displayed beside your slider. You will need this to reset your original resolution in step 7. _____

5. Follow these steps to adjust your screen resolution:

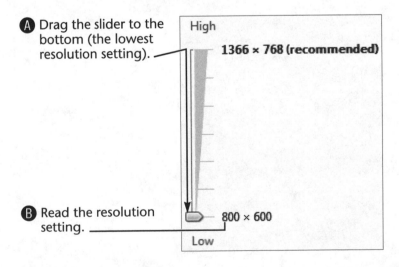

Ⓐ Drag the slider to the bottom (the lowest resolution setting).

Ⓑ Read the resolution setting. _____

6. With the slider at the bottom, click outside the display and then click the Apply (not the OK) button.

The screen may go dark momentarily and then return displayed in the new resolution. Look at the items on the screen. The icons on the Desktop will appear larger than they did previously. Because resolution

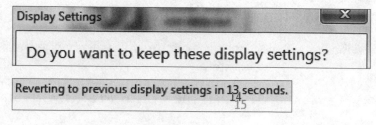

affects the size of objects, changing to a different resolution can rearrange placement of the icons and other objects on your Desktop. Objects may not return to their initial placement on the Desktop if you return to the original resolution.

A smaller Display Settings prompt may appear with a 15-second countdown message notifying you that Win 7 will revert to the previous setting. *Do not* click either button.

7. Wait for the 15-second countdown to run out and let Win 7 revert to your original display resolution setting (if a prompt appeared in step 5).

Win 7 returns you to the Display Settings dialog box.

8. If necessary, reset the resolution slider to the original setting you wrote down in step 3, click outside the slider box, and choose Apply. If the setting is already at what you wrote down for step 3, skip to step 9.

9. Choose Yes if prompted to keep the new resolution setting.

Notice again the difference in appearance as you return to your original resolution.

10. Close [X] all windows.

Glossary

Active   Program currently in use

Aero Interface   The 3D look of some versions of Win 7

Aspect Ratio   Relation between width and height on a computer monitor

Background   Image or color covering your Desktop; also called wallpaper

Bandwidth   Amount of data your Internet connection can provide

Broadband   Generic term for high-speed Internet connection
Example: Cable, DSL

Browser   A program used to access the web
Example: Explorer, Mozilla

Cursor   Blinking indicator where text will appear on the screen when typing (*See also* Insertion Point)

Default Setting   Setting that a computer program assumes you will use unless you specify a different setting
Example: file locations, screen colors, mouse settings

Defragmentation   Reorganizes your hard drive for efficiency (*See also* Lesson 7, Using the Control Panel and Help)

Domains   Divides Internet addresses into groups with common purpose
Example: .com, .net., .gov

Drag and Drop   Method for moving screen objects in Win 7 (*See also* Lesson 1, Getting Your First Look)

Drive   Permanent storage device

Drive Letter   Alphabetical designation assign to storage devices
Example: C:, Removable drive F:

Favorites   Link that you save in your browser

Gadgets   Easy to use mini applications found in Win 7
Example: Clock, Weather, Slide Show

Grayed Out   Object in Win 7 that is lightened in color to show that it is currently not available
Example: button, commands

Handle   Location used for dragging objects on the screen

Hyperlink   Link in a web page that jumps you to another place on the web

Insertion Point   Blinking indicator where text will appear when typing on a computer (*See also* Cursor)

ISP   Internet Service Provider; business that provides access to the Internet

Jump List   List of commands on the Start menu or a program button used to quickly launch related files or features

Libraries Folder System to view and save documents, music, photos, and videos in user and public folders

Mouse Pointer Indicator that moves on the screen in response to the mouse

Operating System Software that manages your computer

Example: Win 7, Win Vista, Win XP, Linux, OSX

Path Shows the location of a file or folder within the organization of a drive (*See also* Lesson 4, Finding Files)

Permanent Storage Device that stores data until erased

Example: hard drive, USB flash drive

Ribbon A program feature used to display program commands instead of using traditional menus and toolbars

Search Engine Specialized page used to find information on the web

Example: Google.com, Ask.com

Shake An Aero feature that enables you to minimize other windows by dragging them side to side quickly

Snap An Aero feature that enables a window to be resized by dragging it to the side or top of the Desktop

Social Media Site Web pages where people and businesses are linked to discuss mutual interests

Standards Uniform look and feel to make the computer easier to use

Tag Keywords that identify a picture

Tree Complete folder structure of a drive

Undo Reverses your last action or command

Updates Changes to a program downloaded from the web

URL Universal Resource Locator; address for a resource on the Internet

Web Common name for the World Wide Web (*See also* Lesson 6, Using the Internet)

Index